START YOUR OWN

FREELANCE WRITING BUSINESS

Entrepreneur
MAGAZINE'S

.:: STARTUP

START YOUR OWN

FREELANCE WRITING BUSINESS

Second Edition

THE COMPLETE GUIDE TO STARTING AND SCALING FROM SCRATCH

The Staff of Entrepreneur Media, Inc. & Laura Pennington Briggs

Entrepreneur Press®

Publisher: Entrepreneur Press
Cover Design: Andrew Welyczko
Production and Composition: Eliot House Productions

This publication is designed to provide accurate and authoritative information in regard to the subject matter covered. It is sold with the understanding that the publisher is not engaged in rendering legal, accounting, or other professional services. If legal advice or other expert assistance is required, the services of a competent professional person should be sought.

Entrepreneur Press® is a registered trademark of Entrepreneur Media, Inc.

Library of Congress Cataloging-in-Publication Data
Names: Pennington Briggs, Laura, author. | Sheldon, George. Start your own freelance writing business and more. | Entrepreneur Media, Inc., issuer.
Title: Start your own freelance writing business / by The Staff of Entrepreneur Media, Inc. and Laura Pennington Briggs.
Other titles: Freelance writing business
Description: Second Edition. | Irvine, California : Entrepreneur Media, Inc., [2019] | Revised edition of Start your own freelance writing business and more, c2008.
Identifiers: LCCN 2019006976| ISBN 978-1-59918-645-0 (alk. paper) | ISBN 1-59918-645-4 (alk. paper)
Subjects: LCSH: Advertising copy. | Small business—Management.
Classification: LCC HF5825 .P346 2019 | DDC 659.13/20681—dc23
LC record available at https://lccn.loc.gov/2019006976

Printed in the United States of America

23 22 21 20 19

10 9 8 7 6 5 4 3 2 1

Contents

Chapter 3

What Life Is Really Like as a Freelance Writer 35

Chapter 4

Business Basics 45

Chapter 5

Launching a Freelance Writing Business 57

Chapter 11

Chapter 12

Chapter 13
Coaching and Mentoring Your Way to Success........ 161

Appendix
Freelance Writing Resources...................... 167

Glossary 171

Index 173

Preface

Have you ever wondered how all of the books, magazines, marketing copy, and websites you encounter each day get written? Does every business have an on-staff team of writers to create the words you read each day? Who writes all of this information? The answer can be found in one word: freelancers. A great majority of the content we read each day is often written by people you never see in a traditional office. Freelance writers are everywhere and work everywhere—from home offices to coworking spaces. And the more information is shared widely (thanks, internet!), the more businesses need good writers to craft messages in a way that reaches the widest audience and converts most profitably. The timing has never been better to start your own freelance writing business.

That said, starting a business always comes with challenges. If you've always loved reading or writing and wondered if you had what it takes to write professionally, be prepared for regularly confronting obstacles and finding ways to maneuver around them. The more you're prepared for this, and have the right tools to support you, the more successful you'll be if you're considering a career as a freelance writer.

Start Your Own Freelance Writing Business, Second Edition will help you understand and adapt to those challenges with resources, tips, stories, and useful information about what it really means to own a freelance writing business managed online.

Whether you studied English, communication, journalism, or a related field (or you're making a lateral move from a related industry), the opportunities to make money online as a writer are wide open. For example, think about how often you consume information you find online. Someone has to create all that content. And as claiming a corner of the internet becomes a more important marketing goal for companies of all sizes, opportunity is knocking for those who have a way with words. Learning how and why online content marketing has changed the landscape for freelance writing will position you to decide whether or not you want to try your hand at wordsmithing.

From figuring out whether you have the skills to sell words as a part-time or full-time venture to discovering the most common types of writing most likely to sell to creating a pitch and work samples and where to find clients, *Start Your Own Freelance Writing Business* is designed to give you a window into what a freelance writing business really looks like.

What This Book Offers

Start Your Own Freelance Writing Business is an easy-to-understand, introductory, and nontechnical approach to the world of online freelance writing. This book teaches you what's required to launch and excel in a business like this and how to leverage the fast-changing pace of technology to grow your business in a way based on the freedom and flexibility afforded by freelancing.

This book will teach you how to:

- ▶ Assess your freelancing skillset.
- ▶ Determine the best way to position your business to clients.
- ▶ Research the most profitable freelance writing opportunities.
- ▶ Create a series of pitches that convert to profitable client relationships.

▶ Set up a work environment that allows you to maximize productivity.

▶ Use freelance job sites to your advantage so you can build a strong client base.

▶ Master the art of time management so you meet deadlines every time.

▶ Market your business in multiple channels to grow and scale your business.

Most importantly, you'll get an inside look at the freelance writing business and related tips of a multi-six figure online freelance writer. By reading this book, you will immediately benefit from that extensive experience to launch your own freelance writing company. So what are you waiting for? The time is "write" to start your own freelance writing business!

Freelance Writing Today

Have you always loved writing and reading? Perhaps as a child you dreamed of becoming a professional writer but somewhere along the way lacked the tools or the confidence to pursue this as a career.

There's good news for you—the digital freelance economy has made it easier than ever to launch a career as a freelance writer with little risk involved. Using this book, you'll get a better understanding of what it looks like to be a freelance writer online today and whether this might be a fit for you.

Even if you ultimately decide that freelance writing is not for you, your time and financial investment will be minimal. Compared to the massive costs associated with launching a more traditional business, freelance writing carries little risk if you have a source of full-time income. In short, it's the perfect side hustle.

Because this startup is low-risk, it's a good idea for prospective writers to initially dip their toes into the freelance waters and not rely on it for a full-time source of income. While many freelancers do write full time, others spend years testing the freelance writing business model and charting their monthly income before they feel comfortable making the leap. We've approached this book with these concepts in mind to help you get a good look at what it's like to be a part- or full-time freelance writer. Using the business know-how from the staff of Entrepreneur and the personal stories, tips, and tricks from my own freelance life, you will get a holistic look at the business from the inside out. If you view this as your chance to explore freelance writing and try it part time, you will either be inspired to grow your venture further or decide it's not for you. Both decisions are powerful going forward.

As for me, Laura Pennington Briggs, I started my freelance writing career out of necessity. I had burned out of my teaching job and knew I didn't want to work in education any longer. My boyfriend at the time (now my husband) had been placed on leave without pay by the military until his new position opened. There were many different avenues out there to earn extra money. As a person in graduate school at the time, however, I'd received a lot of feedback on my writing in the months before launching my freelance career. I figured this was the existing skillset I could build upon the most quickly, so I began my hunt for advice with a Google search: "how to become a freelance writer." There were so few tools, and many of the things I found were extremely dated and not related to the online freelancing market. Many things I learned were trial by fire as I moved from building a part-time freelance writing business to scaling it full time.

Those lessons have been incorporated into this book so you'll be able to hopefully skip some of the more painful ones, learn from common successes and mistakes, and get a perspective on the pros and cons of working as a freelancer.

tip

Think about why you want to become a freelance writer. As you go through this book, determine whether the benefits and challenges of working as a freelance writer line up with your expectations.

Freelance writing is not for everyone. But for those who fall in love with it, it can be an excellent and creative way to make a living. Thanks to the internet, you can manage your freelance writing business from anywhere in the world and grow it to the point you want, whether that's a part-time gig to help you accomplish some financial goals or as a full-time career.

Demand for Writing

It might seem like a dream come true to work as a freelance writer; you've always been good with words, and you'd love to be a paid professional wordsmith. The good news is that breaking into this career has gotten much easier for potential freelancers in recent years, but you'll still need to have a good grip on what's required and have a lot of stamina to consistently pitch your services. If you're willing to push through your launch, you might discover that you've found a side hustle or career you really love.

According to the 2018 "Upwork Freelancing in America Report" freelancing is on the rise across many categories (upwork.com/i/freelancing-in-america/2018). Freelancers can be virtual assistants, translators, transcriptionists, graphic and web designers, web developers, marketing experts, writers, editors, and more.

Each year, Upwork (the biggest job board site in the world for connecting clients with possible freelancers) conducts a study to better understand how many people are opting out of the traditional workforce either to freelance as a side hustle or to create a full-time career.

While Upwork considers the experiences of freelancers overall, the news is good for writers as well. According to the report, key statistics about the state of the freelance market include:

- ▶ Freelancers contribute an estimated $1.2 trillion to the economy.
- ▶ More than 57.3 million people freelance.
- ▶ The majority of workers in the U.S. will be freelance by 2027.

Other studies show the same promise:

- ▶ The "HubStaff 2017 Freelancing Trends" (blog.hubstaff.com/2017-freelancing-trends) study found that freelance writers make up over 12 percent of the online freelance market.
- ▶ According to the 2016 McKinsey Global Institute study, "Independent Work: Choice, Necessity, and the Gig Economy" (http://bit.ly/2HSPHfX) up to 70 percent of freelancers are independent contractors "by choice."

► Twenty-one percent of full-time independent contractors make over $100,000, and that number is expected to grow, according to the 2018 "State of Independence in America" (www.mbopartners.com/state-of-independence) study.

Clearly, the freelance writing market is popular right now, so don't wait too long to get started!

What Is Freelance Writing?

No how-to guide about freelance writing would be complete without a good explanation of what freelance writing is and what makes it different from other pursuits.

In general, freelancers are independent contractors who work with companies or individuals on a retainer or as-needed basis. In the U.S., contractors are treated quite differently from employees. There are a good mix of freelance writers in the U.S. who might work on numerous projects at the same time as a contractor as well as writers who are "on staff" workers, meaning they function day-to-day as a regular employee but get paid as an independent contractor.

This book covers how to land freelance, contract-based assignments, not a full-time job as a staff writer. During your time working as a freelancer, you might have companies offer you a full-time position as a W-2 employee, but this means you are not a "freelance" writer.

If you've ever had an image in your head of a starving artist who can't make ends meet on one end of the spectrum or the fictional *Sex and the City* character Carrie Bradshaw somehow making enough to afford a private apartment in NYC writing one column a week for a newspaper, know that reality is somewhere in the middle for freelance writers. Since there's so much flexibility afforded to freelance writers, you'll find these contractors working many different business models that are best suited for their individual needs and style.

Freelancers are hired by clients to do specific work. Under U.S. laws this means that the freelancer maintains control of their schedule and how the work is completed. A client might give a contractor some directions, but a true "freelancer" most likely wouldn't report to an office from 9 to 5. The freelancer would maintain control over their working environment but would have a contractual obligation to meet the specs of a particular job. Some of these jobs might be "one and done," but others will involve ongoing retainer work.

Simply put, a freelancer has a responsibility to review instructions, sign a contract, then complete a requested piece of writing work. Once the terms of that contract are complete, the freelancer is paid by submitting an invoice.

tip

Try to find some online resources about companies that have chosen to outsource to freelancers. Once you get a better perspective on why they'd consider freelancers, you'll find it easier to speak directly to their needs and concerns.

While some of the specifics of working as a freelancer will be explored later in this book, it's important to know upfront that freelance writers are not employees. This means that your clients don't have a legal responsibility to pay you a salary, provide you office space, or give you benefits. This can actually be used as a way to convince clients who planned to hire full-time workers that they should work with you instead.

Clients like to work with freelancers because they have specific or short-term needs for which it wouldn't make sense to hire an employee. In other cases, they know they can save money by working directly with an outside contractor expert. They won't have to spend time training this person on the writing craft because freelance writers come prepared and experienced. The client gets the benefit of working with a true professional without having a legal obligation to this contractor as an employer would an employee.

Freelancing is not for everyone. The very ebb-and-flow nature of freelance writing means that you should come to the table hungry. You must be ready to market yourself, prepared for the ups and downs of owning a business because you are an entrepreneur and willing to live with the pros as well as the cons of freelance life.

Before you launch your freelance career, it's important to know the ways you can earn money as a freelance writer. Having a realistic perspective of the kind of writing that sells will help you narrow your focus and choose a handful of project types that appeal to you.

Types of Writing People Will Hire for Most Often

If you take a random sample of freelancers, you will find that you likely have a relatively even split of generalists, or those who work on a few different types of projects in different industries, and those who are specialized or operate within a particular niche.

There is truly something for every writing interest in this business. You might be drawn to a particular type of writing, or you might want to think it over as you read through the rest of this book.

tip

You don't have to commit to one industry or type of writing as you launch. One of the best things to do is see what you gravitate toward, then get some experience to decide whether that writing is a fit for you.

There's no rush to pick something and stick with it now, but another section of the book will introduce you to some of the most in-demand writing types. Check out Chapter 2 to learn more about the various types of freelance writing.

Why People Struggle with Writing Things on Their Own

Many people struggle with writing the kinds of copy they need for personal or professional reasons. You'll find clients who have different motivations for hiring a freelance writer and plenty of clients who don't realize the benefits of working with a freelancer until you explain it to them.

The sooner you can understand these different motivations and pinpoint them, the easier your sales conversations will be because you can directly speak to client concerns. These people are your prospective clients, and it's well worth considering why they might be in the market for a freelance writer.

There are three reasons why most clients consider working with a freelancer: lack of confidence in their own writing, lack of time, or an interest in partnering with an expert. You'll find clients who have a mix of primary motivations, but understanding where the client comes from helps you direct the conversation in your favor.

The first reason why a prospective client would hire a freelancer has to do with lack of confidence on the client's part. While clients might be hesitant to state this outright, many people are not confident that their writing style or ability will match up to what's required for success today, especially in the online space.

▶ Identify a Client's Pain Points

Most clients will give you a sense of their reasons for hiring a writer in your initial conversation. This is a major reason why the whole purpose of sending a pitch is not to land a client directly but to open the lines of communication. As they respond to you and hopefully schedule a call, you'll discover that client's pain points. These pain points are very useful for directing the conversation and proposal. When I pitch attorneys, for example, I do so knowing that most of them are extremely busy and don't need one more thing to worry about. All my positioning relates to how my expertise gets them the most traction with minimal time investment on their end. That approach appeals to their day-to-day pain points and increases the chances of a conversion.

As a reader yourself, you already know that the ways you consume information online are different from what you expect from an article in a printed magazine. For some clients, this is a big factor in the decision to outsource freelance writing. If they need to appeal to an online audience but are not sure how to do it, it's much easier to hire an experienced freelancer to get the job done right.

Attorneys are a great example of this. While most attorneys have outstanding writing skills, they apply their knowledge in a particular way in terms of writing legal briefs for the court. The jargon and phrasing used in legal documents, however, does not resonate well with a general audience. Attorneys might recognize that they have a great ability to wordsmith a brief or a petition, but that same finesse does not come across in their web copy, brochures, and blogs. That's why they'll hire a freelance writer.

Other clients might not be confident in their writing ability. They might have been told they have room to improve or that their writing is confusing. These clients will be very hesitant about making a good impression in written materials and will be more than happy to pass this off to a professional. Another subset of these clients are editors looking to have different perspectives incorporated into a digitally or traditionally published magazine.

There's a strong chance these editors have their own writing skills, but they want to include the insights and different writing styles provided by a variety of freelancers. Although I have chosen to focus on digital freelance writing because it is easier to break into and more consistent in terms of revenue, magazine writing can be another way to expand your writing expertise, and you can read more about some aspects of it later in this book.

Another popular reason why a client would consider working with a freelance writer is lack of time. Successful business owners in particular often have enough on their plates, and as the company grows and regular branding and content production move front and center, these overwhelmed business owners cannot take on one more thing. This group of clients includes those who might have a good writing background or a way with words, but for whom the time dedicated to writing is not the most important driver in their business or schedule at this point in time. Although these clients are most likely to be concerned with whether you can adapt their tone and voice in your writing, they are often easy to work with because they prefer independent freelancers who can get the job done with little direction.

Still other clients simply want to work with an expert. They might have the time or writing ability to succeed, but they also know that their work might miss some of the important details required to make maximum impact with each individual piece.

Freelancing Online: Why Technology Helps You as a New Freelancer

In the past, if you wanted to launch a career or side hustle as a freelance writer, you'd have to invest a great deal of work into developing query letters, unique story ideas likely involving interviews, and a master pitch list of publications that might consider your work. It was a purely print route.

While freelance writing for magazines and newspapers is still a popular niche for writers, working online as a freelance writer is often easier and faster. To illustrate the difference, let's walk through the typical process for pitching a print magazine and working on an article for one so you can see how it is different from landing freelance work online.

To start with, you'd need to have a good list of prospective magazines accepting freelance work. Plenty of magazines have downsized in recent years, and most operate with a smaller budget and have in-house writers with busy schedules. While there are plenty of magazines still outsourcing work to freelancers, it's more competitive than ever.

You start the process by getting a list of every magazine accepting freelance work, which would likely be found in a book like the *Writer's Market*. You could also have personal contacts at a magazine or use an online list of those publications accepting freelance articles.

Then you would need to spend some time reading past issues so you don't suggest any articles that have previously appeared and to get a better sense of the type of work that the editors like. You'd also have to figure out how to get over the "clips" hurdle. Editors will want to see examples of your talent, but at the beginning of your journey you'd be stuck in a "chicken or egg" scenario because no one will have hired you yet so you don't have clips, and you don't have clips because no one will hire you. Once all these materials are gathered and reviewed, you've only accomplished one step of the process.

You then use all this research to start crafting the perfect pitch, which you share in a query letter. Many of these query letters today are sent online, but you can still see how you would invest quite a bit of time in this process before even knowing if the editor was open to submissions, had already filled that issue, or had any interest in your article. While some of those pitches might have landed, many would not. If you got a pitch accepted, you'd then learn more about deadlines, length, and other expectations. You'd write the work, turn it in, then wait for feedback. It could take well over a month to get squared away with a final version and more time to get paid. And remember, this is all a best-case scenario assuming that your pitch landed, an editor hired you, and there were no other delays!

Now that's not to say that you can't also do magazine article writing. If you feel called to that, certainly look into it. But as you can see, it's quite hard to break into, and it also means that unless you're in a constant cycle of creating and submitting pitches to an editor, there's little chance for recurring work. Each month you'd have to start fresh chasing down leads and coming up with ideas that might not go anywhere.

The Benefits of Freelancing Online

There are several major benefits to working as an online freelance writer in comparison to magazine article writing:

- ▶ You can define your own schedule.
- ▶ You have better turnaround time from landing the gig to completing it and getting paid.
- ▶ There are lower barriers to entry; it's much easier to land work quickly.
- ▶ The project often requires less work or no interviews, and you don't have to build a series of clips to succeed.
- ▶ While you might still have "lost time" doing research or pitching in the online freelance writing world, there's a greatly reduced investment of your time and energy.

Let's take a closer look at some of these benefits.

Define Your Own Schedule

One of the biggest advantages of working as an online freelance writer is that you can work anywhere in almost any time zone. Sometimes a client will want to ensure you work in a time zone compatible with them so you can schedule the occasional phone call, but others won't care. This is ideal for a freelancer wanting to work nights and weekends while at a day job or dealing with other responsibilities.

If there's anything in your life that makes you want to have or need to have a flexible schedule, freelance writing is perfect for this. If you like working on your own time rather than sitting at a desk between particular hours defined by your boss, and you are capable of bringing that deadline-driven or goal-setting nature to the table, you could be really successful as a freelance writer because you can say you have those basic skillsets and you're self-disciplined.

Sometimes there are days when there's a lot on my plate as a freelance writer. I have to get up earlier or I have to work later or I have to adjust my schedule for other obligations. If you're a parent, have another job, are going to school, or have medical issues, being able to work on your own time is a great benefit of being a freelance writer, but you've got to know how to parcel that time out and to use it effectively to stay on top of those deadlines. If you're too loose with your schedule, you'll really struggle as a freelancer because you'll start to miss deadlines and your clients won't want to work with you.

But if you love the idea of a flexible schedule or if you've had that in a past job and it really appealed to you, a freelance career could be right up your alley because most clients do not care when you do the work—they care that you turn it in on time. They don't care if you work at 5 in the morning or10 at night.

Low Barriers to Entry

One of the biggest advantages of pursuing a part- or full-time career as a freelance writer is that the low barriers to entry make this a great opportunity to try with very little investment or risk on your part.

Assume that you're not experienced enough to make it in the freelance writing world.

Consider that plenty of freelance writers don't have English-related degrees, time spent on a college newspaper, or any other writing experience. They have a love of words and are likely avid readers, but too many people hold themselves back from making a splash as a freelance writer because they assume they don't have enough of the basics to succeed. Far too many would-be writers cut themselves off at the pass because they don't have clips or professional writing experience.

Clips, while still important in the magazine and newspaper writing world, are not as relevant in online freelance writing. Most clients who hire you want to use the work under their own name, and, therefore, understand why you might not have a byline or past work directly connected with your name. You will still need work samples, but these do not have to be published clips. If this has been holding you back from launching your freelance writing business, congratulations—you don't need any clips or a byline to prove your worth with online freelance writing. Many clients ready to outsource their writing needs care mostly about whether you have the general writing skills and ability to meet deadlines. You can learn more about creating samples and an online portfolio in Chapters 5 and 8.

Low-Risk Startup Investment

A great reason to throw your hat in the ring as a freelance writer is that there's so little risk involved. In comparison with the costs associated with launching a traditional business, it's much easier to become a freelance writer. You need very little capital, if any, to get started with your freelance business today.

No business loans, no dipping into your savings, and if you don't like working as a freelance writer, you're not saddled with debt or physical assets you'd struggle to sell. Freelance writing is low-risk because you probably already have most of the technology you need to get set up today. You'll need a computer, an internet connection, time in which

▶ Freelancing Freedom

Increasingly, people are turning to freelancing not just for income purposes but for a more flexible way to earn a living. People with chronic health issues, parenting or caretaker responsibilities, or those who change locations often will find that freelancing suits their needs better than a traditional job. As a military spouse, freelancing allowed me to take my career with me no matter where my better half was stationed.

If you struggle with working on someone else's schedule, freelancing enables you to choose your working hours and build your business around your needs. Although remote work has become more popular, many full-time remote-work opportunities require you to be at your home office during certain hours. If that's not a fit for your life, freelancing could be the solution while providing learning opportunities and the chance to work with amazing clients all on your own terms.

to market your business, speak with clients, and complete work, and a separate business bank account if you intend to make more than $600 in a given year. Make things easy on yourself and set up that business bank account now just in case. More details about that are explained in Chapter 4.

Since I ran my freelance business as a part-time venture for the first year, I can confidently say that if you decide you don't like it, it will be easy for you to "close up shop." You're also welcome to continue operating your business at the part-time level forever if you want, or you can choose to scale it to full-time status. This flexibility is one of the biggest reasons I chose and have stuck with freelance writing for so long.

Know Your "Why"

Business moves quickly online today, which is one the reasons it's so easy to launch your career or to scale it. With the advent of freelance job boards, you can also get a sense of the demand for certain types of freelance writing projects before you start. In comparison, you might have to spend weeks or months pitching to magazines before you get a sense of which clients might be interested in working with you or how competitive the market is. You'll learn more about freelance job boards and how to use them in Chapter 8.

Many new freelance writers are starting this career on the side while they have a day job or after they've left an unfulfilling job. The mental state of balancing your freelance writing business alongside the exhaustion of other life demands can be a real challenge.

Before you get started with your new business, write down your "why." Your "why" could be something like:

- ► I'm working to pay for a great vacation for my family.
- ► I'm working to get more creative energy.
- ► I'm working because I want more freedom in my life.
- ► I'm working because I want to leave my other job.
- ► I'm working because I want to own my own business.

During difficult or long days, your "why" is excellent for self-reflection because it can bring you back off track if you fell short on your goals. Your why is what drives you, and it should be something that's such a core belief that it keeps you going when the going gets tough.

Once you begin to see results in your freelance writing business, it will be easier to remain focused on your goals. The best way to build a sustainable and valuable freelance writing business is by being consistent. There's a saying that the best way to eat an elephant is one bite at a time. By choosing smaller goals that help push you steadily toward your finish line, you'll rack up a lot of small wins. Those small wins turn into ongoing clients, bigger contracts, and testimonials. But before you start, it's important to get the buy-in of your family.

tip

Set a goal for your freelance writing income, and reward yourself with an important purchase once you obtain it. You can get more excited about meeting your goals this way. If you need a new computer, perhaps land your first couple of assignments, and use that income to make an investment in your business future.

Getting Family Members on Board

There are some people in your life who should be brought into the fold if you're going to make a go of starting your freelance business. Your immediate family members, meaning those who live in your house, should be looped into your new schedule.

I kept my freelance writing business a secret for the first several months, mostly because I was unsure if I knew what I was doing and whether I could sustain it. If you want to test things out, you can keep it quiet from family and friends, too. Even though freelancing and online work have picked up the pace significantly in recent years, some people really don't understand what you're doing.

At the end of the day, it's not your job to convince everyone you're really working, you're doing enough, or freelance writing is a real job. It's your goal to get out there and land clients and to meet or exceed their expectations. Stay focused on your goal while reflecting on the reason why you got started, by setting regular marketing goals, and using a schedule you can work with to leverage your time as effectively as possible.

Not only will it help you focus more effectively during your working hours, but it adds to your general store of support when family members are engaged in your freelance writing business launch. Not everyone will understand what you're doing—especially if you're working completely online. But getting your core family members, those inside your home, to understand that they shouldn't interrupt you is important. You'll need focused time to do research, write and submit pitches, respond to clients, and complete client work. It also makes it more fun if everyone is involved in the launch of your new business and is cheering you on behind the scenes!

To help get your family prepared for this transition, consider discussing the following:

▶ Potential "quiet hours" in which no family members interrupt you as you're working
▶ An understanding of your office location and agreement not to touch or move any materials near it
▶ Plans for child care so you have uninterrupted work time when possible
▶ Clarity on whether you'll be able to take phone calls while working and when your family can expect to hear back from you

The Necessary Mindset to Succeed as a Freelance Writer

As you get your family in the right frame of mind to support you, be sure to get your own thoughts in line to prepare for your new venture. Even if you're not completely confident yet about your abilities or chance of success, you must have the right mindset before you can achieve anything with client pitches or work. For some people, the mindset work leading up to their business launch is harder than other aspects like creating writing samples or making a pitch.

This is mostly because there are a lot of stereotypes about working as a writer: It's too hard to break in, writers don't get paid well, or there's no way you'll make a living working online for yourself.

The emergence of the digital economy has changed all that, but this might still be your first interaction with the millions of freelancers providing creative services to companies of all sizes in many industries. As with any new goal in your life, you will have doubts and might struggle to put yourself out there. You might stumble through your first client call, but consider it a learning opportunity to get better next time. Just like with sports or any other pursuit in your life, practice makes perfect. When I launched my freelance writing business, I hated the idea of getting on the phone with my clients. Now I know that my highest conversions come from sales calls that follow an initial pitch, so it has become my favorite part of the marketing process. You might surprise yourself with what you learn.

To be successful as a freelance writer, you must be convinced that you can do this. Of course, you will experience setbacks, challenges, and clients you don't enjoy working with. But knowing how to navigate those challenges will make you a better business owner and will allow you to grow your company more quickly.

tip

The biggest barrier to you becoming a successful freelance writer is you. The more you feel confident about your abilities, the easier it is to sell your services to clients.

The following mantras might be helpful when your subconscious tries to talk you out of starting:

- ► I don't know everything about freelancing yet, but I'm educating myself and I've learned how to do a lot of things in my life with a little knowledge and practice.
- ► Putting myself out there will teach me a lot about myself, marketing, and my prospective clients. I'll use what I learn to become even better as a marketer and writer.
- ► There are lots of high-achieving freelance writers out there who were beginners once, too. All they have on me is experience, and I'll get there one day!
- ► There's a big reason (or a few of them) that I'm pursuing this career. It's so important to me that I will reflect on it when I feel overwhelmed or challenged.
- ► Every setback is a chance for me to analyze what went wrong and how I can tackle problems like that in the future more effectively. I'll use that information to avoid pitfalls and problems with my business.

There's only one person who can stall out your business or take it to the next level: YOU. This book will help you figure out how to fast track your success.

What It Takes to Succeed as a Freelance Writer

Owning your own freelance writing business requires a specific skill set centered around strong work habits and good communication skills. As with all small businesses, there are plenty of people who try it out, discover it's not for them, and decide to pursue something else. Before you jump in feet first, take

some time to figure out if your skills are tailored to the
needs of the profession for the long term. If you've got
the writing skills, are deadline-driven, and open to constructive criticism, this may be the gig for you. If not, you
may want to take a step back to see if you can improve
in any or all of those areas. Sometimes you can enhance
your skills and become competitive with the direct help
of a coach who can provide feedback on your pitch and
samples; Chapter 13 includes detailed information about
when it makes sense to invest with a coach.

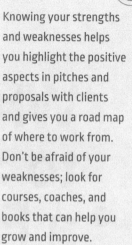

tip

Knowing your strengths
and weaknesses helps
you highlight the positive
aspects in pitches and
proposals with clients
and gives you a road map
of where to work from.
Don't be afraid of your
weaknesses; look for
courses, coaches, and
books that can help you
grow and improve.

   You can certainly still succeed as a freelance writer if
you're willing to work through weaknesses and to make a
commitment to yourself, but being aware of what it really
takes can help you make an informed decision about this
career option. In this chapter, we'll walk through some of
the expectations of the profession and see if you have what it takes to make it in freelance.
Then later, you'll read about the top qualities it takes to succeed for the long term. First,
let's start by walking you through the broad expectations of the profession.

Writing Opportunities

There are many different kinds of freelance writing you could pick up as a side hustle or
career. What follows is a brief overview of some of the different kinds of writing. This is
not intended to be a how-to for each kind of writing, so you should investigate further
when something piques your interest. These categories have been included since many of
them are in high enough demand to work well. There's an art and science to each kind of
writing style below, so plugging some of these keywords into search engines can help you
find examples of what this content looks like or further detail about what goes into these
kinds of projects.

General Copywriting

Clients today often need support with more than one type of writing. From about pages
to social media quips to team member bios and brochures, the term copywriting refers
to general writing projects that capture a company's brand, tone, and voice in a variety of
different kinds of copy and placement. The tone might change from one form of writing to
another, which is why copywriters tend to be versatile.

Search Engine Optimization Blogs and Website Pages

In today's digital age, writing content that matches the search intent of the reader is important. Many companies want to have a prominent internet presence and following, and part of that is writing in a manner that tells the search engines what the page is about. Companies want to rank for particular keywords or in geographic areas (and sometimes both), making a savvy SEO writer someone who has taught themselves the elements of SEO writing. These pieces are usually 300-1200+ words infused with keywords, outbound links, and inbound links. While this might seem overwhelming, learning SEO writing is actually one of the easiest paths to becoming a freelance writer online because search engines require high-quality, fresh content posted on a regular basis, it's a perfect opportunity for ongoing work from the same clients.

The purpose of SEO writing is to establish credibility, to drive traffic and search engine rankings, and to appeal to the target audience.

Newsletters and Email Copy

Email is one of the most powerful tools a company can have. In fact, it's been said that any online business is an email business. Compared with other marketing tools, like social media, email newsletters are one of the few places where clients own the contact information for people who have "opted in" to that list. For that reason, email newsletters and messages have surged in popularity. Most companies contact their email customers at least once a week, which means this can easily be positioned for recurring work.

This copy is usually 300 to 1,000+ words and are designed to share information with a target audience in a personal and meaningful way. The purpose of this copy is to establish a relationship between the writer and reader, to position the newsletter sender as a thought leader or authority, and to sell services or products. Not every email will sell something to the reader. Instead, many companies focus on "nurturing" their lists by providing free value prior to a launch or sale.

Ebooks

Ebooks are long-form pieces of content designed to provide helpful or actionable information. These are often used as free or paid tools to help an audience with a specific problem. Ebooks are usually 2,000 to 5,000 words in a way that builds a value-based relationship with the reader.

Whitepapers

Whitepapers are most popular in the technical or B2B industries as these are a way to showcase trends, research, case studies, and benefits of services or products. These are usually five to ten pages of single-spaced written copy. Most companies who use whitepapers do so because companies can present themselves as experts while highlighting new and existing product/service offerings.

Technical Writing

A great example of technical writing are software manuals and help articles. The purpose of these pieces is to provide step-by-step information with the reader about how to do something. Since technical writing can take so many forms, the length of these content pieces can run the spectrum.

Product Descriptions

These content pieces are most relevant in ecommerce and for companies who provide products. These are short, sweet, and to-the-point statements to describe benefits and features. Product descriptions are usually 30-60 characters or a few sentences. The goal is to quickly capture what a product is, how it's made, or who it's for so a customer can make a download or purchasing decision.

tip

Ask a former English teacher, boss, or friend who has good writing skills to take a look at some of your writing. Choose someone you trust who will give you constructive feedback. This helps you get used to hearing comments about your writing and learning about ways to improve it.

Strong Writing Skills

While you don't need to be an expert on everything to succeed in this field, the most basic tool you must have is great writing ability. If you've had other people tell you that you have a way with words or that they enjoy your writing (whether it's social media, a blog, academic work, or even business emails) you can learn the other skills to succeed with selling your freelance work. But you must be extremely confident in all aspects of writing, including:

▶ Grammar
▶ Punctuation
▶ General tone and style
▶ Ability to write crisp and clean copy
▶ Ability to conduct research and develop it into new material

Investing in online courses about the art of writing and practicing your writing every day will help you finesse your skills, but someone who feels a complete lack of confidence in their writing will really struggle because so many elements of your business are reliant on your writing ability, from pitching to submission of actual work. It's unlikely that someone will hire you and pay you regularly if writing is not one of your strong suits. Unfortunately, not everyone has the general writing ability or grammar knowledge to excel as a freelance writer. If your clients have to spend extensive time editing your work, they'll end up frustrated and may fire you.

Ability to Meet Deadlines

Control your schedule—don't let it control you. In other words, you should have a firm handle on how much work you can realistically crank out in a given amount of time so you can meet the deadlines set forth by your clients. A freelance writer who continuously misses deadlines will run out of clients quickly, but meeting those deadlines and turning out quality work will go a long way toward securing and retaining work.

Remember that you're in control of setting most deadlines, so choose wisely. Don't try to impress a new client by saying that you can turn around a 1,000-word blog post by tomorrow if you need at least two days to gather research and write. It's better to give the client an honest assessment of when they can expect the work than to fall short on a deadline you set yourself.

Occasionally you might run into clients who have unrealistic expectations about your turnaround time. If a client asks if you can do something in a time frame that you find to be stressful or impossible, be up front. These kinds of projects tend to be more stressful anyway, and if the client is under pressure, you won't help things by turning in a project late. Tell the client you'd like to help them but that the deadline won't work. You might find that the client is willing to adjust their expectations, thus reducing your stress and increasing your chances of an effective close to the project.

Some people might have the basic writing talent to wow clients, but they really struggle to meet deadlines or to remain disciplined. And being self-disciplined and meeting deadlines is critical as a freelance writer. You will not be able to keep clients—and won't be able to get them in the first place—if you can't meet deadlines.

If you love working on your own, hated group projects but knew you would do the work and would always meet the deadline, or you never pulled all-nighters to get a school assignment done because you'd been working on it a little bit at a time, you probably have that self-discipline.

Usually when successful writers miss deadlines it's because they don't have the information they need from

tip

Test your deadline abilities. How long does something stay on your to-do list? How often do you tackle something a boss asked you to do on time or early? These are great clues that you have the self-discipline to succeed.

a client. Being accountable to another person will come up a lot in your freelance writing career, and you must be prepared to figure out how to set deadlines, how to tell clients when a deadline they've suggested isn't working, and make sure you keep the client informed if your situation changes. But for the most part, you're working on your own. You're going to get initial materials from the client, then you've got to really take ownership of the project.

If you had to work in group projects in high school, college, or graduate school, you were probably the one that everyone deferred the work to. You were the star of the group because they knew that you would get it done even if everybody else slacked; you were the one who was reliable. This is a key sign you have the necessary deadline-meeting ability to excel as a freelance writer.

► Dealing with Vague Feedback

A few times in my freelance career, I encountered clients who had feedback that was useless. Those two clients prompted me to add an entire section to my freelance writing contracts. Both were different people but said something along the lines of "I just don't like it. Can't put my finger on why."

When someone gives you vague feedback and wants changes, redirect by asking your own questions. Here's an example of how you can handle that.

Freelance writer: "Sorry to hear this wasn't a hit out of the park. However, without specific feedback comments, I'm afraid I don't have any ability to edit. If you could provide some pinpointed feedback, such as specific sections you'd want to be revisited or items to be added, that would give me what I need to make changes."

Sometimes a client who has said something like this to you doesn't realize how vague they've been. Others are trying to scam you and get you to offer a refund (then they'll try to use this piece that was an alleged failure anyways). I now have a clause in my contract that says the client has read my writing samples and agrees that the work they'll receive will be substantially similar in tone and style.

This avoids someone deciding after the fact they don't like your writing style, which is nearly impossible to change. Imagine a client who hates adverbs. They could take one look at my writing samples and see we're not a fit. We're both better off knowing that up front, lest I end up with revisions that will take me a long time. I've found that it's very hard to undo certain aspects of your writing style, so make sure your clients know what your work looks like before agreeing to work together.

If you already meet deadlines for your job or your personal life, whether that means getting your taxes done early or losing 20 pounds by Christmas, you're also going to succeed as a freelance writer because it shows that you regularly set goals and then crush them as you go.

Since freelancers of all types live and breathe by the deadline, you have to be able to manage your own schedule accordingly to meet the deadlines set by your clients. If you've never heard of the Parkinson's principle, you'll want to become familiar with it quickly.

This principle says that the project expands to fill the time to completion. Unfortunately, this principle often means that people waste a lot of unnecessary time. If you have four hours until something is due, have you ever noticed that it takes exactly four hours?

> **tip** ⓘ
>
> Allow prospective clients to review your samples and ask questions about them so you're both on the same page about your overall writing style. Getting specific feedback from a potential client helps you figure out whether this client is the right fit.

Being aware of putting caps on the stages of your writing process can help you avoid the pitfalls of this problem. If you know you need one hour of research to write a 500-word blog, set a timer to stick to it. This will help you meet your deadlines.

As your business grows, you'll be responsible for tracking deadlines for more than just one or two clients. This means that knowing your schedule becomes a matter of utmost importance. Keeping regular working hours and blocking out your calendar with what's on tap will also help when you're speaking with a new client who wants to know your availability. In those fast moments on a phone call, a quick look at your calendar could reveal that you're fully booked. You can use this information to push off the prospective client's deadline or tell them it will be a week or so before you can begin their project.

The Ability to Fly Solo

Being self-disciplined is hard for many people. First, freelance writing can be isolating for some people. If you're used to being in an office where you're interacting with your coworkers all day long and you really thrive on that human interaction, the transition to being a freelance writer, especially if you ultimately make that your full-time job, can feel isolating. Some people really like it. I love it. I don't feel the need to be around other people all the time or to have conversation. I find it distracting, and I work best on my own, in my own environment. If you know you work best alone, you could really crush it as a freelance writer because that's what you'll do 90 percent of the time.

You'll have phone calls with potential clients, progress calls with clients, as well as meetings with other freelancers for networking or mastermind groups, but if you're the type of person who needs that human interaction, you'll need to build that into your freelance business because it's not going to be there automatically.

Accept and Learn from Criticism

One aspect of freelancing I came to appreciate years into the business was my ability to take criticism. Because you're working with clients of various backgrounds, personality types, and demand styles, you will have clients who ask for revisions and edits.

As a writer, you probably have a sense of creative pride over what you've produced. This is a good thing. But allowing that pride to be hurt because a client needs some tweaks translates to you taking things too personally.

Your client might tell you that you need to improve the style, delete entire sections, or retool a project. Within reason, you should be open to making changes because most clients expect it.

Many of them are not attacking your writing personally, but their fresh set of eyes has seen some room for improvement. There might even be times when you don't agree with what a client wants the final product to look like. You can voice your opinion in a nice way, but ultimately, the client is paying you to provide a service, and it's your job to make them happy if at all possible. Listen to their concerns and voice any of your own about what they've asked, then make adjustments as needed.

Here's an example of a perfectly reasonable request for edits and how you might respond if you don't agree with some of the feedback.

Client: "I feel like the opening paragraph doesn't have enough of a 'hook.' I'm afraid a reader won't stay interested beyond that. I feel like the fifth and sixth paragraphs are unclear, and we can we tighten the final paragraph with a better call to action."

Freelance writer: "Thanks for the feedback. Here's an idea I had for a better hook: [Insert Idea Here.] Let me know if you think that's a better take. I've also cleaned up paragraphs five and six. I didn't want your final paragraph to come on too strong, since this is a company newsletter and not an advertisement, so let me know if you think this call to action is a better fit based on that."

Feedback is always hard to hear, even when the client is completely right. If you hear the same things from a number of clients, look for opportunities to sharpen your craft.

When responding to feedback, try to remain neutral if the comments are fair. Add any general notes from the client to a guidelines document if they did not already provide you one. Having these guidelines handy when you write will help you avoid old and bad habits.

Another good practice to help you with feedback is to write the piece, step away, and come back several hours or a day later to review it with fresh eyes. You're much more likely to catch your own mistakes this way.

Be Comfortable with Marketing Your Skills

Some aspects of running a freelance business can be downright scary if you are not hardwired to be an extrovert. Sending pitches, jumping on phone calls, and handling negotiations with people can be difficult. It's also, however, part of the fun process of marketing yourself. If you're scared of talking to people on the phone, you are cutting yourself off from success and the opportunity to fine-tune your sales skills.

Trust me, my first few sales calls went terribly and felt awkward. But each of those was a learning experience that allowed me to boost my on-call conversion rate to 90 percent. If you don't think you can get over the anxiety of speaking to strangers, freelance writing might not be for you. Some practice will help you feel more confident about marketing, but ultimately, it falls to you to do the work even if you feel anxious. Sometimes there's nothing to do but to jump into the deep end of the pool!

As you already read, you'll hear feedback at every stage of your marketing and client process, whether it's solicited or not. Freelance writers who use cold email marketing often report that they get responses like "Take me off your list" or "Never email me again." You have to be able to brush these off and keep going by putting yourself out there. One bad response from a prospective client is not an excuse for taking a week off of your marketing.

It's going to be hard to start a freelance business of any type, but marketing your business will be much easier if you're not afraid of putting yourself out there and talking about how you can help people.

When you're first starting as a freelance writer, you have to do a tremendous amount of marketing. You're going to spend 80 to 90 percent of your time marketing and very little time actually working on client projects. You don't have clients or recurring revenue yet, so you'll spend most of your time marketing, and it can be hard to put yourself out there time and time again and get no response or even hear somebody tell you no.

tip

If you're OK with being a self-starter, but you still crave interaction with others, working as a freelancer in an onsite team or using a co-work space can help scratch that itch.

But outstanding freelancers, the ones who grow their businesses and are able to take off more time and have a lifestyle that that suits their business and vice versa, are the ones who are not afraid to put themselves out there. They hold true to the value that they offer. You're not just interested in talking about how great you are, but you talk a lot about what you can do for a client.

You have to step into the role of being a confident service provider. This will help to convert your clients when they see the value you bring to the table. They will feel confident about essentially paying a total stranger—that's what you are when you're landing clients online—because you possess that confidence and clearly communicate that to them.

tip

Look at your current schedule. Do you have time during mornings, evenings, or weekends to grow your freelancing business if you already have a job or other commitments? Begin to pencil out a tentative schedule of how you can accomplish freelancing tasks weekly.

Be a Self-Starter

To land clients and complete work effectively, you need to be a self-starter and go-getter. Some people thrive in an office or group atmosphere not only because they like the interaction but because it helps them be more accountable. That's great for them—but the freelance life is different.

As a freelance writer, though, you are 100 percent in charge. This has some benefits, such as setting your rates, determining your schedule, and calling the shots about who you work with. But it also has some downsides, because if you can't stay accountable to yourself, your business and your income will take a big hit.

Most people I know who do well as freelance writers are independent people. They prefer to work alone and be self-sufficient and solely responsible for deadlines and deliverables. They also didn't get much out of working in a group environment or even found that having so many people around was a distraction and cost them in terms of productivity.

Knowing which type of person you are is crucial. If you know you work better on your own and trust yourself to do the marketing and client work it takes to be successful, freelancing is a great fit. If you do much better working as part of a collaborative group, freelance writing might be too isolating and too much pressure.

Handle Rejection Well

To be successful as a freelance writer, you have to cast a wide net, because rejection is baked into the formula of freelancing; it's a given. This means that if you reach out to dozens of clients, not all of them will even answer you, much less go through the entire sales process of signing up to work with you. If you don't have the time in your schedule to market and contract ten or more companies/clients per week at a bare minimum, you won't be able to make all the time spent turn into enough of a profit to be worth it for you. Furthermore, your batting average won't be that good, either, because you're not contacting enough clients to convert some of them.

Let's face it—not every boss in the world would want to hire you to work at their office. Likewise, there are many different reasons a client might not be interested in working with you. Sometimes these clients are worth fighting for, but if you get caught up in all the people who've ignored you or told you no, you'll waste a lot of headspace on opportunities that were never going to pan out anyway. In Chapter 7, you'll learn more about the pitching process, what to expect, and how to minimize your chances of rejection.

When I started my freelance business, I sent anywhere from 20 to 35 pitches a day. Many of these went nowhere. Some turned into phone calls. And a few would end up in conversations for work now or down the road. It was hard work to submit that many

tip

If you're drawn to a particular industry or type of writing, there are a plethora of free resources to help you stay on the cutting edge. Podcasts and video channels are a great place to get started. Google Alerts will send you news and blog articles about a chosen topic like "content marketing study" or "copywriting strategy."

▶ What to Do If You Want to Write Creatively

Plenty of writers make a living as creative writers. Some of them write romance novels or flesh out entire outlines for other authors. However, the vast majority of freelance writing projects are in the world of nonfiction. So if it's your dream to write that sci-fi fantasy novel, do it but know that this is different from the many projects you're likely to land as a nonfiction freelancer. If you build your business the right way, your freelance writing projects could help earn you the free time you want to write that novel.

Sometimes a new freelance writer will jump into the market having never written a book before and assume they can be paid $50,000 to craft a book for a client. Has this happened? Sure. Is it rare? Yes. Spend time growing yourself and your talents. You might not even like writing a full-length book once you do it, and the time to find that out is not in the midst of a project with a paying client counting on you.

pitches per day, but it also held me accountable and gave me a lot of practice pitching to and speaking with clients.

Find Extra Time in Your Schedule

To launch and grow a business, you must have some time in your schedule already. It can take time to get traction as a freelance writer, especially since you'll need to ramp up your marketing to land those first few clients. How serious are you about owning a business? There's a joke that entrepreneurs are willing to work 80 hours a week on their own terms instead of working someone else's 40. While you might not need to work 80 hours a week, launching a business is not easy. You'll have to invest time in your own education and marketing. If you only have an hour or two per week, this isn't a good way to spend your time. At that rate, it could take months before you see a return on your investment.

Having five to ten hours a week in which you can work uninterrupted is enough to launch your freelance writing business. Considering how many hours most people spend watching TV, this isn't much to give up to launch a business. In Chapter 3, you'll learn more about what life is like as a freelance writer and a typical schedule.

Whether it's hitting a particular income goal or growing this to the point where you can leave another job, remember that each time you're tired and tempted to put off your work. Breaking down your tasks into small chunks each day makes it doable. That could be spending an hour a day or pitching three companies every single day without fail. Those metrics will help keep you on track and motivated.

Have Patience

Thanks to the internet, it's easier than ever to land freelance writing clients quickly. But every so often I meet a freelancer who expects everything to come to them easily. They say things like:

- ▶ I pitched five clients and got no responses. What am I doing wrong?
- ▶ How soon can I make $10K a month? I just started last week.

Growing a business requires persistence and patience. It will be easier to sell something at a yard sale or on eBay if you need cash today. Building a freelance writing business requires an upfront investment of your time, energy, and confidence. It can pay off in spades later, but it's not a good option to pay your electric bill tomorrow.

Although most freelance writers set reasonable goals, others hope to grow their company faster than they are prepared for. Without much experience, they take the quick-buck route by adding low-paying clients to their schedule, which only amplifies their stress. If your business is built on stressful, low-paying clients, handling many of these at the same time is not worth the extra income if you feel like you're under pressure all the time.

Recognize that not only will it take time for you to build well-paying consistent income but that you'll also have to invest money in your company as you go. More courses, books, coaching, or training might help you get to the next level faster.

Stay on the Cutting Edge

Are you the type of person who loves learning new things and taking on challenges? Freelancing might be a great fit for you. By its very nature, technology is changing all the time. So, too, are marketing methods. Consider the related world of social media marketing; every year new social media platforms will come online, grow, or even fizzle out. Marketers in the online world, including content writers, have to stay on top of trends and research. If you're not willing to put in the time to enhance your skills, you won't be competitive, and your business will dwindle.

As an SEO writer, for example, I'm always watching what Google is doing. I'm seeing what experts have to say about structuring paragraphs for online readers. I'm even reading about how many people support the Oxford comma. I do those things because it's my job to see where I can best be of service for my clients.

▶ The Role of Confidence

When I first started as a freelance writer, I wasn't confident in my skills. I'd never been paid to write a word and I had no idea what I was doing, but I learned as I went and I worked with some great mentors who helped take me to the next level.

You might think that launching your freelance writing career involves a lot of learning how to write effectively, price your services, convert clients, and pitch to clients—and these are important—but a great deal is about confidence. The confidence you bring to the table will not only help you in your marketing but will also help you convert those clients and deliver better results because you feel more confident about what you're doing.

If you'd prefer to learn something once and be done with it, another industry might be a better fit. Writing requires a mix of talent and willingness to learn and grow.

Be a Good Juggler

Be prepared to keep many balls in the air as a freelancer. As a freelance writer, you're not just a creative. When you launch, you're also CFO, CEO, and VP of Marketing. In any given day, you'll be:

- ▶ marketing
- ▶ working for clients
- ▶ answering questions
- ▶ doing research
- ▶ completing administrative work like submitting invoices

If you don't have a system to keep track of all the details, your business will start to feel like more of a headache than a joy.

Remember that as you grow and start making more revenue, you can invest in support like a virtual assistant or software to keep you organized. Before you have enough money coming in, though, it's on you to be organized.

One thing that will help you when you launch is to write down every project as soon as it comes in, then break these projects into smaller pieces: researching, writing, editing, and submitting. Slot each of these into an appropriate space on your calendar so you have plenty of time to complete the project.

It can sometimes feel chaotic jumping from one project to another or hanging up a client phone call and going right into writing mode. As you go along, you'll pick up tricks for running your business more effectively, but rest assured that if you're growing in the right way, you'll always be in uncharted territory to some extent.

Top Five Signs You'll Succeed as a Writer

One of the questions I get most often is "How do I get started as a freelance writer? How do I even know I would be good at it?" You'd be surprised to learn that most of my students and the people I've coached into becoming freelance writers have a problem with confidence rather than talent. They have the talent, but they don't necessarily have the confidence to get started.

While a lot of people can succeed as freelance writers, it's not the right fit for everyone. In this section, you'll learn more about what it takes to succeed. Freelancing is growing faster than most sectors of the work force, and there's a high demand for people who are competent writers, whether it's for sales copy, email newsletters, blogs, whitepapers, even full-length books. If you have the skillset to do the work and you have a lot of the different qualities that I talk about in this book, you're going to walk away with a renewed sense of confidence about launching your freelance writing career.

I've been a freelance writer since 2012. It started as a side gig and quickly grew into a full-time business. I left my day job and started earning more as a freelancer after just three months. In my second year, I started earning six-figures, and my business has continued to grow. Since 2013, I have been fully booked. I share this to explain that freelance writing services are definitely in demand. I've also hired a tremendous amount of freelance writers myself, trained them directly, and served as a project manager and content manager for companies like TrueCar and Microsoft. I've seen both perspectives of freelance writing— pitching my services as a freelance writer and hiring freelance writers. In other words, the demand is there. If you have the talent and you meet the different signs that I talk about in this book, you could make a good living or even a part-time income as a freelance writer.

Most people who are interested in freelancing hear or read a story about someone else's journey that's motivational and inspiring, but they don't know if they have the skills. So they talk themselves out of it before they even begin.

If you possess a lot of these qualities, you should start to feel confident about building a successful business because you have most of the skills you need. To get started, all that's left is the right mindset and toolkit.

There are a lot of different signs that you may be successful as a freelance writer. Here, I've broken it down to my top five. These are qualities that are found in many successful six-figure and part-time freelance writers.

Good Grammar Skills

First, you are really going to struggle as a freelance writer if you do not have good grammar skills. Do you need to be able to diagram a sentence and explain every little detail of grammar? No. You don't have to be a grammarian, but you need to have basic grammar skills.

You need to know where to place punctuation like commas and you need to know how to use present, future, and past tense words and keep sentences coherent before you ever consider a professional career as a writer.

If you really struggle with grammar or if other people have critiqued a lot of your grammar, you're going to want to brush up on that before you ever consider a professional career.

A lot of your clients may not be confident in grammar, or you may have clients who are extremely picky about grammar. For example, you may work with attorneys and insurance professionals who tend to be highly educated and detail oriented.

They are outsourcing because they don't have the time or the interest, but they are definitely going to grammar-check your work. As a baseline skill, you should feel relatively confident that you have good grammar skills.

Your Eyes Are Naturally Drawn to Mistakes

The second sign that you might really crush it as a freelance writer is that your eyes are naturally drawn to mistakes. Are you always spotting other people's errors?

You might notice this on social media, where you see other people's posts, and it drives you crazy that they are never written properly. You might also see it in co-workers' emails, or you might be the person who always finds the spelling error on the restaurant menu.

Maybe you're reading a book and you spot the typo that the proofreader missed or the word that's in the wrong tense. If this is you, you may be more likely to be successful as a freelance writer because you're drawn to mistakes, which means you're mindful of them and you'll be more apt to avoid them.

You're an Avid Reader

The third clear sign that you might be extremely successful as a freelance writer is if you already spend a lot of your free time working with words. By that I mean you're an avid reader. It tends to be the case that people who spend a lot of time reading also tend to like writing and vice versa. As a result, your additional exposure to a lot of written materials has probably taught you a lot about vocabulary, grammar, punctuation, and more. So if you like reading, whether it's email marketing, books, blogs, or ebooks, that's a pretty good indication that you're very familiar with word and sentence structure. This could be extremely beneficial as you prepare to launch a freelance writing business.

You should consider being an avid reader one of the strongest tools in your arsenal because there are so many powerful connections between writing and reading. Ultimately, you're going to be responsible for reading your own work and reading materials from your clients.

No matter what you like reading, if you spend a fair amount of time doing it, then you've probably picked up a lot of skills that will translate well to a freelance writing career. The more you read, the more familiar you'll become with the English language, which can help to position you as an amazing freelance writer.

You've Always Been Told You're a Good Writer

A lot of people overlook the fourth sign: Other people have always told you you're a good writer. Perhaps it's a boss who complements your professional emails, or a professor in college who said you were a great writer.

If other people have already given you good feedback, this is a good indication that you are able to present your thoughts clearly and coherently to the end audience. You adeptly think about the words you're saying, the order you place them in, and how you generate flow throughout a conversation or a written piece.

You Love Problem Solving

Sign number five is you're a natural problem solver. You enjoy solving problems and overcoming challenges. The more you grow as a freelance writer, the more you'll find that some of your clients will turn to you as a strategist and not just as a writer.

They'll be asking you for your input about how to achieve particular goals. I have a client, for example, who regularly asks for my input on how many emails he should send leading up to a webinar series and what the subject lines should be. That's more of a strategy issue; it's sort of a fusion between strategy and writing.

Your clients may come to you with very specific concerns. For example, a client may tell you that people are visiting their website, but they are leaving quickly before they get any value or sign up for an email list. Or they might say, "Our website is not ranking in Google. How can you help us with that?" You may also hear, "Our competitors are outpacing us in the production of whitepapers, and it's hurting our bottom line."

You step into the role of problem solver and strategist a lot. You may be responsible for problem solving before you even start working with a client because you have to convince them that you're the right person for the job.

You're not always going to have every answer, but you're going to have that natural problem-solving ability that helps you to figure out solutions.

What Are the Downsides of Being a Freelance Writer?

When you're thinking about making a career transition or starting a side hustle, it's just as important to consider the negatives of what you're going to do as well as the positives.

It's so easy to find marketing materials about all the upsides of being a freelance writer. But if you're not careful, it's easy to get overly excited about a career that also has its challenges. However, the great thing about freelance writing is that you can navigate these downsides when you understand your underlying mission and your drive to freelance.

As any entrepreneur knows, there will always be negatives in any profession. What's important is whether the negatives work for you.

In some situations, you'll be able to cope with the negatives, overcome them, or, at a bare minimum, accept that they are just part of the bigger journey. But sometimes the negatives will really bother you and far outweigh the positives. For me, a huge negative would be working in an office situation where I'm micro-managed and have zero say over what I do every day. I just sit at a desk between 9 and 5 because that's what my boss tells me to do. That would drive me crazy, so I know that it's not the right fit for me.

There are downsides to freelancing, too. Your job is to figure out if these are things that you could cope with, or will they be a major annoyance? Will you be able to devise a plan to handle them, or go in with an open mind and realize they are part and parcel of being a freelancer?

Let's take a closer look at some of the most common challenges of working as a freelance writer.

You're Going to Be Alone a Lot

It's true. Sometimes being a freelance writer can be lonely. You work often on your own. For those people who don't really want to be around a lot of other people or hear a bunch of background noise, it's perfect. You may be one of those people who are fine being alone and prefer having control over your working environment.

Despite this, you may still want the occasional human connection. If so, there are ways to combat being alone so much, including:

- ► Getting out once a week to work in a coffeehouse
- ► Joining a co-working space
- ► Joining a weekly meeting (in person) with others
- ► Finding an online accountability buddy you can Skype with once a week
- ► Planning podcast appearances or calls with clients

These tips can help you stay connected with your clients or other freelancers in a way that feels natural and still gives you control over your schedule.

Other People Might Not Understand What You Do

Some people will act like you're not working at all. Even though working from home and solopreneurship are picking up traction worldwide, there are still plenty of people out there who are confused and assume you're sitting at home watching Netflix all day.

It's sometimes hard to help family members or friends realize that you're not available all hours of the

tip

Build breaks from your computer and keyboard into your schedule using a timer. This is a great chance to rest your eyes and fingers while also stretching and getting ready for another block of work.

day. There's a fine balance between being able to meet a friend for lunch and having someone get angry that you didn't answer their text message while you were working on a client project.

> **tip** ⓘ
>
> Using bookkeeping software and the right CPA goes a long way toward keeping you organized and making sure you meet your tax obligations.

There's no perfect solution to this. You may have to get more serious with setting boundaries for everyone to understand when and how you'll be able to respond to them. Sometimes all it takes are a few gentle reminders, but in other situations, you might have to put your foot down.

Taking Care of Taxes

If you've been in the traditional employee work force for some time, your employer has taken one of the biggest administrative headaches off the table for you—taxes. If you intend to work for yourself, you'll have to cover your self-employment taxes to make up for the fact that you're not paying into Medicare or Social Security through your payroll. You'll also have to pay your own taxes out of all the income you receive, unless you form a corporation in which you payroll yourself. Even if you do form a corporation, you'll still pay individual income taxes on the amount you paid yourself, but your accountant can help you discuss tax-saving strategies. Either way, you have to take on a bigger leadership role for paying your taxes. Taxes are discussed in greater detail in Chapter 4.

You Will Deal with Bad Clients

While it should always be a goal to work only with ideal clients in your business, that's not always possible. You usually have to go through a couple of bad experiences before you settle on the right people to work with.

When you have a bad client, there are a few things you can do to make this situation easier:

- ▶ Recognize what role, if any, you played in this process.
- ▶ End the relationship as soon as and as professionally as possible.
- ▶ Move on and look to find a better client to fill that space.
- ▶ Apply any lessons learned to your hunt for new clients.

In many cases, there are red flags that we see early on with some bad clients that can help us refine the process of finding better clients in the future. Red flags can include poor directions, lack of communication, a client who pushes your boundaries by trying to reach you too often or calling/texting you without permission, or someone who refuses to stay within the terms of the contract, adding on more work with no discussion or extra pay.

Your Income Will Fluctuate

Think of this one like a game. It's not always possible to predict your income perfectly as a freelance writer, but there are steps you can take to guard against the famine part of the feast and famine cycle.

Here are ways you can handle a fluctuating income:

▶ Focus on netting a particular dollar amount of projects or retainers every single month.

▶ Have an action plan to get freelance writing cash fast when you need it.

▶ Make sure you always have money saved in case of an emergency.

When you're prepared for the possibility that your income might change from one month to another, having these safety nets in place will give you confidence to ride the wave of possible changes.

You Will Type a Lot

It goes without saying that you'll be at the keyboard quite a bit as a freelance writer. This can lead to some painful issues, including eye strain and carpal tunnel. Do your best to take breaks often. Consider getting a standing desk to minimize the pain of sitting all the time.

Take breaks for ten minutes every hour to get a break from typing. Regular breaks and knowing your own limits will help you tremendously as you prepare for a career as a freelance writer.

Now that you know some of the signs you'd succeed or struggle as a freelance writer and some of what it takes, in the next chapter, you'll learn what life is really like as a freelance writer so you can decide if this is still a fit for you.

3

What Life Is Really Like as a Freelance Writer

W hether you're launching your freelance writing business with no other obligations or you only have ten hours per week, the good news is that the work, both in terms of marketing and in completing client work, can be flexible based on your needs.

Many people are able to turn their freelance writing business into a full-time venture. Still others are happy with the part-time income or that their side freelance work fits into their schedule as a parent, employee, or volunteer.

Given these variations, a freelance writing business may look different from one provider to another, but the core elements are still the same. In this chapter, you'll learn more about what it's like to work as a freelance writer and what you can expect when you launch your company vs. years down the road when you're established.

A freelance writer handles many different types of typical tasks over the course of the day. As a freelance writer, you must be adept at juggling your multiple responsibilities to achieve client goals and continue to move your business growth forward.

Some of the key tasks carried out by freelance writers on a regular basis include:

▶ Researching

▶ Communicating about instructions and deadlines with clients

▶ Writing

▶ Editing and proofreading

▶ Delivering work to clients and sending out invoices

▶ Answering questions from clients

▶ Completing revisions for clients

▶ Sending out pitches to prospective clients

▶ Posting content on your blog or your LinkedIn profile to attract new business

All these activities can be extremely valuable for developing your freelance writing business, but all of them are also unique tasks, which is why dividing them and blocking out your schedule is a solid way to accomplish each of your ongoing goals.

In this chapter, you'll discover what a typical day might look like for a freelance writer, how you can expect to divide your time when you launch and grow your business, the value of self-discipline and setting a schedule, and how to set boundaries with friends and family who might have to adjust to your new venture.

A Typical Day in the Life of a Freelance Writer

The truth is that one of the reasons I have loved working as a freelance writer for so long is that no two days are alike. This might be the right fit for you if you love a good mix of variety and stability.

As a fully booked freelance writer, most of your time will be dedicated to working on client projects, but you'll also want to keep an active marketing engine to be as effective as possible. Marketing is a critical component of freelance businesses because

tip

When do you find yourself most focused and productive? If you can, build your freelance writing schedule around that. Night owls love using the evening hours to knock out tasks, whereas early birds will get a lot done in the morning hours before the day kicks off.

it helps you to avoid the feast or famine cycle. Feast or famine refers to the fact that many people land plenty of work, then get lax on their marketing efforts. After they've wrapped up all the jobs associated with those initial marketing efforts, they find themselves in a famine cycle with limited cash flow and opportunities on the table.

Consistent and regular marketing is one of the biggest keys to success in running a freelance business. What follows is a typical day from my schedule as a working freelance writer.

Using Sundays to block out your weekly schedule will allow you to slot in time for every aspect of your business, including marketing, researching, writing, and delivering client materials.

Keeping some semblance of a basic schedule and blocking out your time helps ensure that you won't overbook yourself. Let's walk through a typical day.

Morning

In the morning, take a look at your schedule to make sure you don't have any pressing client meetings that could interrupt the day of work. During this time, you can also respond to any emails that came in from the previous afternoon and focus on one or two key projects.

You might consider batching your work as a freelance writer, meaning that you stay focused on one task a time, such as researching, writing, or editing. Batching your tasks helps keep you on deadline, and the same can be said for the marketing aspects of your business. Since you break down your writing process into various stages of research, writing, and

editing, it's harder to fall behind when trying to stack all of these tasks on top of one another the day of or the day before a deadline. When you batch, you've got forward momentum on that stage of the project and ideally have it spread out over half-days or entire days so that you can limit the possibility of last-minute procrastination which is stressful and can compromise your work quality.

Breaking up client work in the morning and editing it in the afternoon or even the following day ensures that you maximize the chances of catching any errors.

tip

Breaking your work into distinct parts— researching, writing, and editing—helps you write more clearly and fix mistakes more easily.

Breaking up client work into different tasks, such as doing one task in the morning and another in the afternoon helps you increase the chances of catching errors.

Since mornings are usually the most focused periods for me, I do most of my "heavy lifting" during that period as well. Discover when your most focused work gets done, and create your freelance writing schedule around it.

Midday

During the midday portion of your working hours, you can recap what you've already completed in the morning and do another check of your email inbox. This is your first opportunity to see whether any new messages have come in and to prepare yourself for the afternoon portion of your business.

> **tip** ⓘ
>
> Midday lunch breaks work well to get some marketing or client phone calls done if you have a day job.

If you take a lunch break, you can recalibrate between the morning's activities and your next goals during the afternoon period. If you have any client calls coming up, this is also your chance to review where you're at with a project and the agenda for the call.

Afternoon

Some people are more focused in the afternoons. If that's you, you might consider swapping the morning and afternoon schedule suggested here. I reserve my time in afternoons for client phone calls, delivering client work, and administrative tasks, such as sending invoices and verifying that I have the appropriate instructions for the following day. This is because my writing is better done in the mornings, but you might feel differently.

Batching things, including answering all the emails in your inbox that have come in after periods of focused work is one of the most effective tools for staying on top of my inbox while also not getting distracted working on a client project. As I said earlier, one of the big reasons I love freelance writing is that no two days are alike. While I might still be marketing and working for clients each day, I like to mix it up with different activities so I don't get bored. Writing for different clients also adds variety to your day.

Self-Discipline and Working Hours

Now that you've learned what a typical day in the life might look like as a freelance writer, it's important to take ownership over the creation of your schedule and how to stay focused to meet your goals.

The freedom of freelancing makes it easy to think that you can work whenever you want to, right? Although this is true, it's going to require a lot of self-discipline, especially as you move out of a traditional work environment and into a freelance one. Many well-meaning freelance writers struggle to get their business off the ground after they leave a traditional job and don't have a plan in place for that transition.

Suddenly going from an office or another working environment in which you have a supervisor or boss establishing the rules of how you show up and what you do to having the ultimate flexibility in creating and marketing a freelance business is hard. In this section, you'll learn some tips to make sure that you don't get derailed and miss out on landing new clients right away.

One of the most important traits for a freelance writer to have is self-discipline. As a working writer, you will live and breathe by the deadline. Freelancers who don't meet deadlines end up losing all their clients and quitting. Unfortunately, there's a stereotype that writers are flaky, and there are some freelance writers in the marketplace who live up to that reputation. If you don't have grit and relentless self-discipline, you'll struggle with what to do with your time.

How to Set a Schedule for Your New Freelance Writing Business

In addition to writing down your reason for starting your freelance writing business (as you did in the previous chapter), it helps to set a schedule.

If you're like me, one of the biggest reasons you're looking to grow a part- or full-time business as a writer is because you don't like being on a schedule. While you don't have to commit to spending 9 to 5 in front of your computer every day, having clear working hours helps you stay focused and ensures that you can begin stacking up those small wins.

Writing is like exercising: The more you flex those muscles and fit in reps, the stronger the muscle gets. When you first start, the time it takes you to complete a project will seem significant. You'll also be grappling with self-doubt about whether you have what it takes to do well at this. The more that you practice pitching and writing, the more confident you'll feel and the more easily the words will flow.

Since you're just starting to use those writing muscles, try an abbreviated schedule. Trying to sit yourself down and work nine hours on writing tasks if you've never done it before can feel exhausting. More important, if you set such a big goal and don't stick with it, you'll feel like a failure. Small, incremental changes are the best way to work up to being booked as a writer.

When you build your schedule as a freelance writer, it will vary based on whether you have existing obligations (school, parenting, work) that pull away a lot of your focus.

Of course, the hours you have free to dedicate to your freelance writing business will be reduced. However, you can probably find some time at night, on weekends, and in other pockets, such as when you have child care. Once you know all the possible hours you have free, do your best to schedule your freelance writing activities for when you are most focused during those available hours.

Personally, I'm not a night owl. Trying to write during the evenings after a long day of work just made me feel like all my thoughts were muddled. I soon learned that my most focused hours, and also the hours when I produced the most work, were early in the morning. I got up early every day, including weekends, and worked on pitching or client work. For the entire first year of my business, I had a full-time job with hours from 8:30 to 5. I also had night class for my doctorate twice a week, so that meant I had to be really strategic with my time.

You know your body best, so try to mesh up all the open time in your schedule with the time when you're most likely to be alert. I loved early mornings because no one else was up and I could use a lot of my brain power in the 90 minutes before starting my day job, but for you, there might be a critical hour after you put the kids to bed for the night when you can get the most done.

Whatever you decide, set a schedule. Block it out in your calendar as an event. Get the support you need from a spouse, family members, or child caregivers to ensure you have that space.

A sample schedule for someone working a full-time job, in addition to starting their business, could look like this:

Monday, Wednesday, Friday 6–8 A.M.: Marketing freelance business

Tuesday, Thursday 8–10 P.M.: Client work and following up on pitch responses

Lunch hours: Phone calls with prospects to discuss working together or instructions

It's going to take time and work to get where you want with your freelance business. Is it doable, however? Yes. I've known moms of multiple kids under the ages of five and long-haul truck drivers who fit their freelance business into their schedule the best way they knew how. A key to this is setting goals that are just slightly out of reach, commonly known as stretch goals.

For example, your stretch goal might be to reach ten new potential clients every single week. Since you won't convert all ten clients, or even likely get half of them to a phone call or the proposal stage, it's important to pick a big enough goal so you have the chance to reach the number of clients you need.

> ### ▶ Should Your Tell Your Employer About Freelancing?
>
> Unless you envision your freelance work interfering with your ongoing job, I don't recommend telling your current employer about your freelance business. It might lead them to think that you'll be less focused or that you're putting a plan in motion to leave.
>
> When I started writing, I found it was easiest to fit in my freelance writing business around my existing day job. I left my employer out of it. Your employer might accidentally discover your gig, however, if you're friends on Facebook or connected on LinkedIn. If you intend to keep this private for now, keep that in mind and be mindful of how you share your marketing materials.
>
> Ultimately, if your freelance writing business doesn't detract from your work responsibilities, it's really none of your employer's business what you're doing with your free time.

Still, reaching out to even two new prospects every workday feels like something you can accomplish. And over time, reaching ten new people each week can lead to a lot of warm leads and current clients on the line.

A schedule helps you accomplish the marketing goals you need to speak to enough clients to begin getting conversions, but it also prevents you from getting distracted or talking yourself out of your freelance business. For a lot of people a lack of confidence gets them off track without a schedule. Keep pushing at it and remain consistent, and you will see results.

Bear in mind that when you start your freelance writing business, and any time when you try something new like bringing on more clients, there will be an adjustment period. Be kind to yourself; trying something different is equal parts exciting and confusing. Soon enough, you'll have your feet firmly planted under you to serve your clients while also growing your business.

Dividing Your Time as a Freelance Writer

Speaking of schedules, one of the most important distinctions between a new freelance writer and an existing one is the amount of time spent on marketing activities vs. the time spent doing client work. As an established freelance writer, I spend the vast majority of my time meeting current client deadlines, attending meetings with clients, and discussing additional opportunities for their content marketing.

In the beginning of your freelance writing business, however, you will spend approximately 80 percent of your time marketing the business and only 20 percent or less completing client projects. This is simply because you have not built up your client roster yet and need to drum up a lot of business.

If the thought of spending so much of your time marketing for prospective clients scares you, rest assured that this proportion of time dedicated to your business will shift over time, but that marketing will always remain one of the cornerstones of being able to draw in new clients and build long-lasting relationships.

There are many different ways that you can effectively market your freelance business, which are discussed later. You must be prepared, however, for the concept that you will need to be marketing every day.

When I launched my freelance writing business in 2012, I spent four out of every five hours working on my business in direct-marketing activities. That included speaking to prospective clients, posting content designed to draw those prospective clients into my world, and having initial conversations with potential clients.

Not every client you communicate with or send a pitch to will end up working with you. This is why casting a wide net and being regularly engaged in marketing activities are two of the most important things you can do to grow your business. Marketing is largely a numbers game, and finding marketing methods that work for you and convert at the highest possible level is the best way to leverage your time.

At the launch of your business, other critical marketing activities, such as the creation of your writing samples, the drafting of your pitch, and the generation of a marketing plan must all be complete before you can start marketing your freelance business. The only way to draw in prospective clients is to have a pitch that piques their interest in speaking with you further, then having writing samples that back up the quality of your work.

Although you may need to spend several hours creating these foundational materials, the same pitch and writing samples can be used to land you gigs over and over again. When I launched my freelance writing business, I had never been paid to even write one word before. I had never served on a college newspaper, studied communication or English, or had any semblance of a professional writing career.

Since I had no samples to launch my freelance writing career with, I created them on my own. The three samples I created during this initial marketing process were used to land dozens of different gigs, all in my ideal client niche.

This made it easy for me to leverage my time and the marketing materials I had put the most effort and energy into creating. Since you're going to be spending such a significant portion of your time marketing your business, it's essential that your pitch and your writing samples are the most effective calling cards possible. These may be the only materials on which a new client bases their decision to hire you.

Later in this book you'll find greater detail about how to develop effective pitches and writing samples that can land you work again and again. You can learn more about writing samples in Chapter 5 and more about effective pitches in Chapter 7.

Why You Need a Marketing Schedule

As is mentioned above, you'll spend most of your time as a new freelance writer prospecting for clients. To ramp up your new business, the best thing to do is to create a schedule for your marketing. Otherwise, it's easy to feel overwhelmed and fall short landing clients. Since marketing is the most important aspect of your new business, a schedule keeps you accountable.

One of the easiest ways to stay on top of your marketing goals in your freelance business is to make a time-based commitment or a pitch-based commitment. Having specific numbers to reflect on gives you something to work toward and can also help you redirect your efforts if you've fallen off track.

Pitching is a numbers game, and it may take you many different pitches to realize what works and what doesn't. You will be in an excellent position to start marketing yourself after you have created these critical marketing materials. Establishing a numerical goal, such as five hours per week or sending three to five pitches per day, is one of the most consistent ways to stay on top of your marketing goals.

As you develop a numeric goal, be realistic. While it might be exciting to think about the prospect of sending 50 pitches in a week or carving out 15 hours in your schedule to market your freelance writing business, far too many new freelancers shoot for the moon and are never able to keep up with the rigorous schedule they've established.

► Carving Out Time for Marketing

When I started my freelance business, I was working a full-time job. That meant I had limited hours in the day to market my freelance writing services. I showed up to work one hour early and pitched myself for that entire hour before my co-workers arrived, then added in another pitching session during the lunch hour from 12 to 1. This was the only time I had during the day to pitch my freelance writing services. But because I did this two hours a day, five days a week, that was an additional ten hours of marketing efforts. All those little chunks of time added up and helped me grow a sustainable business. Set realistic goals that help you accomplish what you want to achieve without adding too much stress.

Even 30 minutes a day of marketing activity can make a difference, but only if you do it every day. Remain committed, and don't get deterred from hearing "no" from prospective clients. Eventually, you'll convert people into paying customers and develop those trusting relationships that can lead to future work, referrals, and testimonials.

> **tip** (i)
>
> Block out your freelance work hours in your physical or digital calendar. Treat it as a part-time job or obligation that you take seriously.

The only way to be effective as a freelancer, whether as a beginner or as an advanced freelancer scaling your business to six figures and beyond, is to remain consistent with your marketing. As a fully booked freelancer writer, I still build in marketing time to my business, because it ensures that I never have a dry spell, or worse, slip into feast or famine mode.

In the beginning of your freelance writing business launch, it will seem as though all your efforts are spent on marketing, but this is the greatest way to build momentum. A small bit of work accomplished every day and every week will begin to compound on itself and set you up for success in the future.

Make a numeric goal that you can stick to. Realistically, how many minutes or hours per day can you dedicate to marketing? And what will be the most efficient way to schedule those particular minutes to get the most out of them? You might need to, for example, remove all distractions from your desk, phone, or mind during the time you market.

Now that you've got an idea of how to build out your schedule for writing and marketing tasks, it's time to dig into the nuts and bolts of getting this freelance life off the ground. In the next chapter, we'll walk you through some of the basic startup tools you'll need to ramp up and open shop.

Business Basics

It's important to consider that you're operating a business—even if it doesn't involve a storefront or office full of employees. The sooner you begin treating your company like a business, the easier it will be for you to make the important decisions you must be able to make as a freelance writer.

If you have a hobby, you'll soon notice that you treat this hobby differently from your business. We often have hobbies in which we invest time or money without much concern for "return on investment." You might simply enjoy the activity. Running a business, however, requires a shift in thinking. The sooner you begin treating yourself like a business owner, the easier it will be for other people to take you seriously, too.

In this chapter, you'll learn how to set up a professional workspace, how to choose a legal structure, what licenses or details you need to have organized to launch your business, and more.

Setting Up a Professional Workspace

One of the big benefits to working as a freelancer is that if you have a laptop, you can work anywhere. The downside to this, however, is that it's easy for your entire home to start feeling like a workplace or source of stress. For the purpose of minimizing this and keeping your focus, it's a good idea to have a dedicated workspace, even if you don't have a lot of real estate to choose from. A hallway desk, a small corner of a guest room, or even a repurposed closet can help you get into the zone for working on your business.

A dedicated workspace makes it much easier for your brain to snap into "work mode" when it's time to market your company or to do client work. Your family or roommates will also have to adjust to you working from home, and having one place where you work makes it easier for them to respect the boundaries of you working on your projects and business.

Try to keep a clutter-free desk with only the most important elements of what you need to do your job. Some of the most crucial aspects of such an office or space include:

▶ A comfortable chair
▶ A desk with enough space for your computer
▶ A printer and/or scanner
▶ A nice desk light
▶ A place to store pens, staples, and extra computer paper

These extra supplies make it easy to print documents and to scan them back to your clients faster. Documents like nondisclosure agreements and contracts are discussed in Chapter 10 of this book.

tip

No matter where you choose for your physical workspace, stock it with necessary supplies and make sure it's organized. It's much easier to check into work mode when your workspace is welcoming and clean.

Choosing a Legal Structure

One of the decisions you must make during your business startup is choosing an appropriate legal structure. You might change your business structure over time, but to start out, following is a brief overview of the different types. For more detailed information on choosing the right legal structure for your business, check out *Start Your Own Business* (Entrepreneur Press, 2018).

Sole Proprietorships

Many freelancers launch their business as a sole proprietorship because it is a fast way to begin freelancing operations, requires no special approval, and is easy to change to another business form later. This is ideal when you are just starting out and are perhaps unsure whether your freelance business will be a success. Keep in mind, however, that the tax hit is a big one, especially if you bring in a solid income. You will have to pay estimated taxes each year and account for the correct withholding amount. The estimated taxes must be paid quarterly if you make more than $600, and you will need to set aside money to make these payments based on your sole proprietorship income. On the upside, you have flexibility and little paperwork to file with the exception of estimated payment vouchers and taxes. On the downside, you will not enjoy the same legal protections that you might with a more structured business model.

Partnerships

Partnerships are another option. However, this structure is uncommon for freelancers, especially those just starting. It is suitable only if you have completed some assignments for another freelancer nearby with a similar or complementary style. Formal partnerships, especially those that legally bind each partner, typically come later in a freelancing career and only if you intend to partner with another freelancer on an ongoing basis and each have a stake in the business together.

On the other hand, informal partnerships such as those in which freelancers subcontract work, are quite common and can occur anytime the primary freelancer acquires too much work or needs help getting a portion of a project completed. Subcontracting is not a legal partnership as far as ownership of a freelance business is concerned. It is merely a method to get work completed for a client.

Before entering into any binding partnership, it is important to put together a legal written partnership agreement. The agreement should include such things as how the partnership will be dissolved, what happens to existing clients, and who is responsible for specific tasks. You must also fully understand your liabilities and responsibilities as a partner. Be aware that in the eyes of the law you can be held responsible for your partner's actions. For example, you and your partner may agree to pay taxes, but if your partner fails to do so, you could be held liable and responsible for any unpaid amount.

Corporations

Corporations are sometimes created by an active freelancer. All the money received from the freelancer's clients are paid to the corporation, and the corporation then dispenses funds. In essence, you, the freelancer, become an employee of your own corporation. Just like an employee, you receive a paycheck, and taxes are deducted from it.

The advantages of this structure are that you may end up paying less in taxes and the corporation can purchase items you need for your business. Some of the disadvantages are that you have more forms and paperwork to file with the IRS and your state and local tax authorities. Never form a corporation without consulting your attorney and tax advisor. Fully understand your rights, duties, and obligations.

Some potential clients are more likely to use your services if you are a corporation rather than a sole proprietor. The reason is that they can contract with you as a corporation and not as an individual. This way, they can avoid any pension rights, workers' comp, or benefit claims. As your freelance business grows, consider this a reason to form a corporation.

Most freelancers start their business as a sole proprietorship. It's fast and easy and takes little time. Forming a corporation costs money, requires approval from the state, and necessitates advice from experts.

Secure a Tax Identification Number

To get paid by a client, you must provide them with a tax identification number. For most individuals, this is a Social Security number, but with identity fraud on the rise, it doesn't make sense to list your SSN on your invoices. You can solve this problem by applying for a tax identification number from the IRS. For sole proprietors as well as other legal entities, this is an employer identification number (EIN).

You can use and apply an EIN even if you have no employees. See IRS publication 1635 for information about understanding your EIN. Visit the IRS website (www.irs.gov) to obtain an EIN. After all the fields are completed on the online form, preliminary validation is performed, then a provisional EIN is issued to you.

Your EIN can be used to open a bank account, apply for a business license, make a tax payment, or file a paper tax return, but it will not be available for use on the IRS electronic system, such as e-file or EIN matching, for up to ten days. You can also receive an EIN by completing form SS-4 (Application for Employer Identification Number) and faxing it to the IRS for processing. The IRS fax numbers are provided in the instructions for form SS-4. Visit www.irs.gov/forms-pubs/about-form-ss-4 for more information.

Determine If You Need a Business License

Depending on your location, you may be required to obtain a business license. Some locales require them, and others do not. A quick telephone call to your local municipality, city hall, or county courthouse will tell you if you need a license. Many times, freelancing businesses are not required to be licensed. However, this is not universal, and you could be breaking the law by offering freelancing services without registering or obtaining a license. Find out what your local regulations are, then follow the law.

For example, California charges freelance residents (or those doing business with California clients) an $800 franchise fee. Your state could also charge similar fees. You can find out by visiting the website of your state's franchise tax board.

Set Up a Business Bank Account

You might be curious about what steps you need to take before you go all in with your new freelance writing business and which ones you can wait some time to establish.

Bear in mind that at the time of this printing, the IRS considers anyone who earns more than $600 in a calendar year to be operating a business rather than a hobby. Depending on when you launch your freelance writing business, you could quickly surpass this goal.

This makes it critical that you be prepared to operate your freelance writing venture as a business from the moment you begin. One of the most important ways to do this is to establish a business bank account. It can be very confusing from a tax and business operation perspective when you comingle your funds. This can be a big mistake that can make it more difficult for you to sort out data and evidence down the line if you are audited. Establishing a business bank account at the outset will make it easier to run your venture like a true business.

Why Have a Business Bank Account?

One major reason to establish a business bank account is to ensure that others view your company as legitimate. Some companies might prefer to write a check to your business account, rather your personal one. But you may also be able to receive checks made out to your personal name if this is associated with your business at the bank.

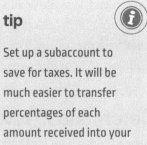

tip

Set up a subaccount to save for taxes. It will be much easier to transfer percentages of each amount received into your tax subaccount.

Another key reason why you need to establish a business bank account is because not all of the money you earn is your own. You will need to pay taxes on your income. When you have a full-time job, your employer deducts Social Security and Medicare taxes from your paycheck.

As a freelancer, however, taxes are your responsibility. Establishing a bank account for your freelance business and subaccounts where you can set aside money for taxes is strongly recommended. This also helps to show the IRS and other state revenue agencies that you are operating a business legitimately and professionally, should any auditors come knocking.

Trust me, it's much easier to establish a business bank account from the get-go and deposit all your money there, parsing out funds for yourself, taxes, and business-operating expenses rather than attempting to do this several months in. Some freelancers are caught off guard by how quickly their business grows, putting them in a difficult situation with regard to taxes and business planning if they hadn't considered it before.

Planning for Taxes

You should retain the services of an experienced and knowledgeable accountant. While many accountants are familiar with filing taxes and even in individual state tax requirements, you should retain someone who has experience in representing self-employed individuals or home business owners. Speaking from personal experience, this makes a big difference in getting help when you need it and exploring all possible avenues for tax minimization.

Hiring an experienced accountant who understands self-employment taxes, the freelancing market, or homebased business ownership, will help you leverage the power of all the deductions to which you are entitled. The first year I filed my taxes, I was receiving a W-2 as a full-time employee, but I also had supplemental freelance income. My accountant's lack of knowledge about homebased business ownership cost me thousands of dollars in deductions that I could have claimed. Don't make this mistake. Seek out the services of experienced tax professionals.

When searching for an accountant, it is also important to find out whether they offer audit protection services. As a freelancer, you'll certainly need your accountant for more than filing your annual taxes. Your accountant should be knowledgeable about different

▶ **Accountant Advocacy**

Since starting my freelance business, I have received multiple letters from the IRS, which were a result of their confusion over me having multiple clients and receiving so many 1099s. Having an accountant who provides audit and IRS protection services means that I simply scan this material and my supporting evidence and send it my accountants, who are much more familiar with and successful in handling disputes and corrections with the IRS. Now I don't stress out when I receive one of these letters, and it has helped ensure that I have the appropriate evidence, bank statements, accounting software printouts, copies of 1099s, etc. should I need to provide it quickly. When you try to take on the IRS yourself, it is much more difficult to establish a paper trail or to get in touch with the exact person you need at this massive agency. Accountants, however, interface with state revenue departments and the IRS on a regular basis, which can make your defense much more effective.

types of business structures and the amount of taxes you pay with each, as well as the personal liability you face as a business owner. Your accountant can also become a crucial source of support if you receive letters from the IRS such as those where your income was miscalculated due to multiple 1099s counting the same money, an internal review of your tax file that claims you owe more money than paid, or requests for more documentation to support your returns.

Accountants are also knowledgeable about the different avenues available for filing your taxes and for protecting yourself should you face an unexpected tax surprise. Accountants can help build a case for you to fight off additional penalties or fees in certain situations and can recommend how to get on top of an outstanding IRS or state revenue debt sooner rather than later. Do not make the mistake of trying to use software tools to manage your taxes on your own. The minute that you start operating a business, things become much more complicated, and you are also a higher audit risk because of the many deductions business owners claim.

How to Set Aside Enough Money for Taxes

Your individual tax rate and the amount of business expenses you have will all influence the total amount of taxes paid. In the best-case scenario, you will set aside more money in your tax account than you need. Set up a separate bank account or a subaccount where you can automatically transfer a certain portion of every check, deposit, or payment that you receive.

When it comes time to pay your quarterly estimated taxes, which are the taxes you pay four times a year based on your estimated income, it will be much easier to pull this money out. You can wait until the end of the year to pay your taxes, but you may incur additional fees and penalties. Having a business bank account, transferring a portion of your income for every payment you receive, and paying your quarterly estimated taxes will significantly decrease your chances of an unexpected tax bill .

Many experts recommend setting aside 30 percent of everything you bring in for taxes if you are a sole proprietor. If you exceed the amount that you need to set aside for taxes, such as in a quarter where you had significant business expenses but still set aside 30 percent of your overall revenue, you can use this to fund additional expenses that you have been saving for, to pay yourself a bonus, or to continue saving for any unexpected tax problems in the future. Having more money than you need set aside is always a better problem to have than scraping to set aside enough money.

Now of course, it's unlikely that you will need to pay 30 percent of your taxes. However, most people are not prepared to pay self-employment tax to cover their Social Security and Medicare contributions. So setting aside 30 percent is a good barometer. If you discover this is too much or not enough to cover your tax obligations, adjust as needed, but be consistent with the amount of money that you transfer to this subaccount or separate business bank account. Thirty percent is just an opening recommendation. You should consult with your accountants to identify if you need to be setting aside more.

Common Deductions for Homebased Business Owners

As with all things related to taxes and financial planning, your individual experience may vary, but homebased business owners and self-employed professionals are entitled to a broad range of business deductions that might apply to your situation.

Below is a brief list of some of the different items that you might be able to deduct in your business:

- ▶ Internet expenses based on the portion of your internet usage that is for business purposes
- ▶ The purchase of a new computer, specifically for business purposes
- ▶ A business phone line that you use only to receive and make client calls
- ▶ A portion of your mortgage or rent based on the size of your home office
- ▶ Mileage on your vehicle to and from client meetings
- ▶ Costs associated with purchasing courses and books and attending conferences directly related to your freelance writing business

▶ Subcontractors who you allow to work on your clients' freelance writing projects or subcontractors who are directly helping you grow your business, such as a virtual assistant who sets your appointments and sends invoices

▶ A portion of your utility costs based on the size of your home office

As a mentioned above, these are just a few examples of items you can deduct. Finding an accountant who has an exhaustive list of the types of deductions you are eligible to take might open your eyes and save you hundreds or thousands of dollars come tax time.

From the moment you begin earning money in your freelance business, it's a good idea to track your income and expenses. This will help you make decisions about growing your business in the future and how to properly account for your expenses and taxes.

Preparing for Expenses

When you start your business, you'll have very little in the way of expenses, such as your internet costs, your computer, and possibly some minor expenses for a job board site like Upwork or some other marketing methods. As your business grows, your expenses will grow.

The first expense I had in my business, outside of my job board site, was a virtual assistant. As your company expands, it will become harder to operate as a solopreneur who can handle everything. This is one of the biggest challenges that freelancers must account for because it can be hard to see that these are investments and not just expenses. If you have questions about whether an expense qualifies as a deduction, ask your accountant before you make the purchase.

Examples of expenses for a newly launched freelance writing business might include:

▶ Job board site memberships or software programs ($10 to $50 per month)

▶ Internet expenses

▶ Computer purchase and maintenance

▶ Business cards

▶ Website hosting (if you have a website)

While it can be hard to imagine investing money into something when you haven't generated any revenue yet, consider that you'd need to invest a lot more cash up front to own any other kind of business. In comparison with launching a retail store or other brick-and-mortar

tip ⓘ

You'll find it much easier to track your expenses from the moment you launch, rather than trying to pore over old receipts and notes. Set aside a weekly or monthly time to keep track of new income and expenses. Being in touch with your numbers will keep you organized year round.

company, testing out a freelance business comes with much less risk due to the lack of startup materials needed.

At the outset of your launch, it's a good idea to remain focused on keeping your expenses as low as possible. As your income begins to grow, you can consider investing in software tools like paid invoicing tools, task or project management systems, and paid contract software or people to help you spend more of your time with money-generating activities such as a virtual assistant or a business coach.

Consider Outsourcing

When you start, you're the CEO, CFO, VP of marketing, and accountant. Over time, however, you can outsource some of these activities to a virtual assistant so you can focus on the tasks in your business that make you the most money and leverage your time effectively.

Examples of tasks you could outsource to a virtual assistant include:

▶ Researching companies for you to send pitches to
▶ Editing your freelance writing work to ensure it's proofread properly
▶ Managing your invoices and bookkeeping
▶ Responding to emails and meeting requests
▶ Managing your website
▶ Sending pitches on your behalf (either fully writing them for you or sending your drafted pitches)

Over time, you'll want to keep track of the tasks you do most often in your business and decide whether these should be outsourced. You might even outsource client work to other freelance writers if you have more than you can handle.

Selecting Software

As mentioned earlier, you need only minimal supplies to work and launch your business as a freelancer. However, here are some great software programs to run your business:

▶ *Grammarly* (www.grammarly.com). This is a grammar and spelling tool that catches many of your common mistakes. The free version is likely sufficient for your needs.
▶ *The Hemingway app* (www.hemingwayapp.com). Use this app to help identify tweaks and mistakes in your writing to enhance your overall writing style.
▶ *Copyscape* (www.copyscape.com). This tool will ensure that your work is completely original. It looks at all information on the internet to verify that you haven't

copied anyone else's existing work. Duplicate websites are not favored by Google, so all work you create should be original.

▶ *NovusScan* (http://terranovuslabs.com/novusscan/). Currently in beta version, this software ensures you don't copy your past work. You can upload a past version of your writing, and the software compares it to your new work. This is really important if you write a lot of the same content for similar clients. I use this when I'm writing a client's website so I don't accidentally repeat myself.

▶ *Invoicely* (www.invoicely.com). I love this free program that allows you to send PDF versions of invoices to your clients and track what's been paid and what hasn't. Paid versions include Wave or FreshBooks, but I don't think they're necessary for a new freelancer dipping their toes into the water.

▶ *PayPal business account* (www.paypal.com). PayPal is an easy way to collect payments and have a paper trail for auditing/tax purposes, but there are fees associated with using it. However, if you do a lot of business through PayPal, over time you'll become eligible for PayPal's working capital-based business loan.

▶ *GoDaddy Online Bookkeeping* (www.godaddy.com/email/online-bookkeeping). For an affordable cost, you can connect your business bank account or PayPal account.

Your business situation might be unique. This is where a consultation with a business lawyer and accountant can open your eyes to other issues you should consider as you launch your business.

Launching a Freelance Writing Business

W hen it comes to launching a freelance writing business, most people quit before they get started, but gaining some confidence and knowing the appropriate steps you need to take can give you the encouragement you need to start your freelance writing career today.

Most people fall for the myth that says, "I don't have any experience so there is no way I will be hired as a freelance writer." However, I launched my freelance writing business with no professional training, certification, or degrees, and I am largely self-taught.

Your purpose in purchasing this book might have been to figure out whether a freelance writing business is for you. One of the reasons that I love freelancing is because it is much easier to open a freelance business with limited resources and time. Opening a traditional brick-and-mortar business would require months or even years of research, identification of capital sources, and testing your marketplace.

You probably already have most of the tools you need to launch a freelance writing business, and for many people, it's about overcoming low confidence rather than the practice of working as a freelance writer that blocks them from getting started.

Now that you have taken stock of what it takes to make a successful freelance career and you've gotten a handle on what to expect, you have most of what you need to launch your freelance writing business. So what are you waiting for? Let's launch!

You can launch your business with a few key steps: researching your marketplace, creating your samples, discovering your unique value proposition, and creating your pitch and marketing plan for building your business. You'll also need to determine the time you have available to build a business and to set realistic goals.

Researching the Marketplace

You cannot launch a freelance writing business without knowing whether there is a demand for your services. You might have all the passion in the world for writing about a highly niched topic, but if there are no clients to hire you to do this work, you will be unlikely to build a sustainable freelance writing business.

Doing your research in advance helps to clarify whether there are industries requesting freelance writers who are within your area of expertise or passion and who can clarify how you might narrow down your overall marketing plan. No one should launch their freelance writing business without first conducting research.

It is strongly recommended that you look at some of the freelance writing job boards listed in the resources section of this book to get a better handle on the types of work and industries in which your ideal clients are working. Bear in mind that not every client will post their job on one of these job boards.

Some of the most common job boards include:

► Upwork
► Freelancewritinggigs

▶ Writer's Weekly

▶ Guru

▶ Freelancer

▶ ProBlogger

tip ⓘ

Always research the demand for jobs but also your competition. Who are the most successful writers on these platforms? What do their profiles have in common? What kinds of writing samples do they have available to view?

The highly technical nature of whitepapers, for example, means that many freelancers who solicit work as a whitepaper writer form a direct connection with the company rather than applying through a job board.

That being said, job boards can be a great place to find out whether people are seeking freelance writers in a particular field or writing within particular project scopes.

Typing in keywords such as "SEO blog writer" or "whitepaper writer" can give you a sense of the clients seeking relationships with freelancers today. If you do your research and discover that the industry or niche in which you thought you wanted to write doesn't have much demand on these job boards, all hope is not lost. You need to continue your research process to verify your results.

One key way to do this is by forming relationships directly with these companies by connecting with their marketing officers on LinkedIn or reaching out to digital marketing

▶ Jack of All Trades?

When I launched my freelance writing business, I considered myself a jack of all trades and marketed myself that way. That meant that I took on blog writing projects, ebooks, brochures, whitepapers, and even sales copy projects across the board. If a client was interested in my writing style, I was happy to provide them with a quote.

I learned that marketing myself as a jack of all trades was a mistake when I worked for a client who wanted me to write about software technology. This wasn't in my wheelhouse, and the final product wasn't something I could be proud of or that the client could use. I knew immediately that based on this experience, I would not take on another project in software technology.

Even though that experience cost me time and money, and required the client to go back to the drawing board to find another freelancer, it was a valuable experience. I realized what I didn't want to do and how I needed to target my marketing efforts in the future.

agencies who might have already formed relationships with these types of ideal clients. You might not be able to break into your ideal type of writing project or work directly with your ideal client until you have gotten some experience.

Don't anticipate that your first client or couple of clients are going to be the dream people you hope to work with. A big part of the process involves deciding what you do and don't like, and you might not realize the types of writing that you don't enjoy doing until you have had the opportunity to do a project.

This research process is highly valuable for giving you a basic idea about whether there are companies out there you would like to work with. Remember that not every company will be interested in hiring freelancers.

Some might require a long proposal process during which time you educate them about how to work with a freelancer. Others will be closed off to the idea entirely as they may have in-house teams or established agency relationships.

Some may have freelancers working on their projects already but do not have a space for you at this point in time. This is why I often recommend that new freelance writers cast a wide net and pursue research into several different types of writing opportunities before committing to establishing a marketing plan. Once you get some practice and experience, you'll be in a better position to decide how to proceed.

Create Your Samples and Discover Your Unique Value Proposition

Creating your work samples is crucial. You might want to conduct research into other freelance writers who specialize in the type of projects or industry that you do, just to give you a sense of what else is out there.

In addition, you must know your unique value proposition, which is what you—and only you—can offer the customer.

While every writer can produce high-quality work, what is it about the experience of working with you that makes you different from other writers or from the client's in-house writer? It could be that you deliver on time every time, or you guarantee originality, or maybe you have 20 years of experience in the field you are writing about.

Think about what makes you distinct from other writers and how you can stand out from the crowd. This is especially important as you launch your freelance writing career, since you may be using marketing methods like job boards, in which you will be directly competing with other freelance providers. Your samples should communicate your overall writing ability and be aligned with the type of projects the client is looking to hire.

This is not to say that you need to write a 50,000-word book to be hired as a ghostwriter, but someone who is hiring ghostwriters will take you much more seriously if you at least have a few sample chapters of a book that you can show. Blog writers should have blogs, whitepaper writers should have a sample whitepaper piece, and so on. It is not a good idea to use something you have created for your job in the past if you do not have legal permission to do so.

Freelance writers should create their own samples from scratch. Far too many would-be freelancers get hung up on the fact that they were never professionally hired to create these samples.

Rest assured that I landed dozens of freelance writing gigs my first year with three blogs that no one ever paid me for. I wanted to show my ideal clients my overall writing style and what a typical blog from me might look like, and those three samples landed me gig after gig without a problem.

This should be the same approach that you take for creating your own samples. If you want to be a blog writer, think about some of your favorite blogs that you have read from other people.

Conduct research and get a sense of the general length, tone, and style of these pieces, then create something similar. Perhaps, for example, you recently read on a friend's blog a great piece she wrote about how to break your smartphone addiction. You might approach

▶ Showcasing Your Samples

Publish your samples far and wide. Use them on job board sites, use your own website if that's in your skillset, or use an online portfolio platform like Contently. Note that Contently largely prefers bylined clips on websites, so the word document you created might not work there. Building a small microsite or portfolio page is relatively simple, but there's also no need to invest in the big expense of a custom website when you're just launching. Most clients want to see samples of your work so they can review your talent and skill. Most writers see little to no difference in publishing actual sites vs. using Google Docs or a Dropbox link, unless the client specifically asked to see published samples. Since most online freelance writers are ghostwriters who agree not to share past client work, it's unlikely you'll have many published website articles with your name attached to it. For six years, I've used a Dropbox folder where I house PDF versions of my samples and have never had an issue with this. Choose something that you—and clients—can easily access. This way, you can direct them to the samples most relevant to the work or concept you're pitching at the time.

this topic in a different but related way by talking about how to make sure that as a self-employed person you don't spend too much time sitting all day. These are the pieces that can give you inspiration, but you should never attempt to copy anyone else's work.

Most writers err on the side of sending too many samples or using a portfolio site that has ten or more works. Most clients will never read all of these, so sending too many can overwhelm the client or cause them to look at the first one, which might or might not be your best work. It shows thought and strategy to send no more than three samples most in line with the kind of work you're pitching to the client and explaining why.

Stating something like "I've attached this humor piece I wrote because it captures a lighthearted tone about an otherwise difficult topic, which I think would be a great approach to take with your content, too" helps a client see that you're already thinking ahead. This is a psychological way for the client to begin imagining you on their team already.

Create Your Pitch/Marketing Plan

This is often where many freelance writers fall off entirely because they get consumed by the details of what they should charge for a particular project before they even have any prospective clients on the line.

Creating your pitch and marketing plan is always the step that should be done after you create your samples because the very practice of creating your samples and identifying your unique value proposition can open your eyes as to what makes you different when compared with other writers.

Your pitch and marketing plan should be something you can stick with. If you are employed in another industry and have outside obligations, it's unrealistic to commit 20 or 30 hours per week toward building your freelance writing business.

However, having a number in mind, be it the number of pitches you'll send each week or the number of hours you'll spend building your business, can help you work toward the accomplishment of growing your business and doing so successfully. Many freelance writers fall off if they send their first couple of pitches and don't hear back or have a client who tells them they are not interested.

Here are some tips for creating a marketing plan:

- ▶ Be prepared to cast a wide net with your weekly reach-outs or pitching. Plan to contact far more people than you'll convert. Sending 25 pitches per week is a great way to get the ball rolling.
- ▶ Set aside specific hours in your calendar for marketing work. When you first launch, I recommend five to ten hours per week.

▶ Stick to your goals and hold yourself accountable; post your weekly pitching goal in a note on your desk or in a spreadsheet where you track your progress.

▶ Do as much research as you can about specific marketing tips for your chosen platform (i.e., LinkedIn or cold emailing).

▶ Keep notes about what pitches and marketing methods are most successful for you. Your top two marketing methods should be the ones you focus on.

It can take dozens of pitches for someone to generate that conversation with you, which is why many freelance writers pursue job boards first since the turnaround time can be much faster once you learn the ropes of that particular job board and have established a good sample and overall pitch.

You're likely to use several different marketing methods when launching your freelance writing business until you find one or two that resonate most closely with success. This can include freelance job boards, in-person networking, LinkedIn and other social media, emailing potential clients directly, and more. The specifics of how to land clients online and offline is reviewed in greater detail in Chapter 8.

Should You Start a Side or Full-Time Business as a Freelance Writer?

Perhaps one of the greatest benefits of becoming a freelance writer is the enhanced flexibility this career option provides. When you launch, your goal might be to scale to a full-time level over time, or you might have a part-time income goal in mind. Understanding how these two are different and what's right for you is important.

I balanced my freelance writing career on a part-time basis for over a year while working at a full-time job. Many people choose to use their freelance writing career as a supplementary source of income, and others will choose to leave their full-time position to pursue freelancing on a full-time basis.

What follows in this chapter are some recommendations about making that decision between starting a side or full-time business and how to make the transition from being a part-time freelance writer to a full-time one.

Which Option Is Right for You?

As a new freelance writer, you don't need to commit to working full or part time right away. Plenty of people find fulfillment working as a freelance writer part time, whereas others discover their passion and want to commit to this as their full-time gig. You can shape your freelance journey to your individual goals.

Most freelancers start part time until they can scale up their business with more clients. Getting those first couple of clients will probably be the hardest. It can take a lot of marketing time to secure those first few projects, but you can also use that experience to decide how much of your schedule you can dedicate to freelance writing over the long term.

Set Financial Goals to Reverse-Engineer Your Business Goals

Having a number in the back of your mind is extremely effective when building your freelance writing business. It's easy to become reliant on the income that you generate from your traditional job, but if you do not have financial goals for your freelance writing business, it's easy to fall off on the daily pitching and marketing work required to build a sustainable freelance writing venture.

Financial goals allow you to work backward from what you want to earn and the time that you have available. Remember it can take some time to get traction as a freelance writer, so it's unrealistic to assume that spending two hours a week is going to generate hundreds or thousands of dollars per month.

Setting a smaller financial goal, such as $500 or $1,000 a month, and working backward to determine how much time you need to spend marketing to achieve is a great place to start. Most people underestimate the amount of time required to build a successful marketing scheme.

Whether you are relying on job boards, cold pitching, or other forms of marketing, it can take 10, 20, or even 30 hours of work to land a client. For some people, this number is more or less.

> **tip** ⓘ
>
> Set "stretch goals" for your freelance writing business. Setting goals too high sets you up for feelings of failure that make you want to give up. Stating that you want to earn $5,000 in your first month is a lofty goal. While possibly achievable, it won't be possible for the majority of new writers. Set a goal that feels doable, but slightly out of your comfort zone. A great goal to set before moving on to others is $1,000 a month. Then you can set your sights on bigger plans.

Understanding the time that you have available will influence your ability to generate business and stay consistent with your plan, but knowing the number that you intend to earn in the back of your mind gives you clarity about whether you are on track with your goals or if you need to turn up the heat.

Working Full Time vs. Part Time: Employee Benefits 101

One of the biggest distinctions between working as an independent contractor vs. working as an employee for someone else's company has to do with the provision of benefits.

There are trade-offs to working as a freelance writer, and the biggest one of these has to do with providing benefits and ensuring that you pay all your taxes appropriately.

As an employee, your employer most likely takes care of the benefits for you and withholds taxes from your pay, which you may or may not get back come tax season. As an independent contractor, you must be prepared to factor into your budget self-employment taxes, health insurance costs, and more, since these will not be provided by your clients.

Remember that while this might be the downside to you and something you need to have a plan to address, it can be an advantage to discuss this with your prospective clients.

Knowing they do not have to hire a full-time in-house employee and can instead leverage your talents without paying for your benefits can be a powerful marketing tool.

One of the most difficult aspects of launching a freelance writing business is figuring out how much you need to set aside for self-employment taxes and health insurance. Health insurance is a significant expense for many freelancers. If you have access to a spouse's plan, this might be one way for you to cover your insurance costs. Do some research in advance, and use calculators online to understand what you need to set aside.

Since you will be paying for your own taxes and providing other benefits for yourself as necessary, your financial goals for your freelance writing business might need to be several hundred or thousand dollars higher than you anticipate. You want to build the flexibility into your budget of preparing in advance to pay for these prospective costs and concerns.

Should You Write in a Niche?

Have you ever heard of a niche? In the world of freelancing, a niche is a way to narrow who you work for or what you do. You'll find some freelancers who lament "Ditch the niche!" and will instead encourage you to work for everyone and anyone. There's a downside to that, though, because if your clients or projects are too different, you can get overwhelmed or exhausted. Niching is not right for every freelancer, but focusing on just a handful of industries has made a world of difference in my business.

A niche is a way to differentiate yourself from being a generalist. Most people start their freelance career as a generalist because they don't know what their niche is, and that's fine.

You can honestly work as a generalist for years and years, or you might find over time that patterns emerge and you want to focus on particular types of projects or to work for specific clients, and that's essentially working within a niche.

You will see people across the board: those who have a niche and those who don't, and you will hear advice from people who tell you that you should never work in a niche. But be wary of writing something off until you've tried it.

tip

You don't have to choose a niche, but, as their business grows, many writers may start feeling overwhelmed if their attention is spread across too many projects and they don't narrow in on some type of favorite project or client type. Even if niching is not right for you now, consider returning to this chapter in the future to review the material again.

There are exceptions to the rule. I have been working in a well-defined niche now for six years, and it's been instrumental to helping me grow my business very quickly. That doesn't mean I can't take projects outside of that or work with people outside of my usual industry—I do. But having a niche has opened a lot of doors and has positioned me as an expert with my clients.

In this chapter, you'll learn more about how to break down what you do as a freelancer and how that relates to niching. Then you will learn how the pros and cons of niching affect what you do on a day-to-day basis, how you sell to clients, and whether it is better for the clients if you specialize in their industry or in the type of project that you provide.

Ways to Niche as a Freelance Writer

There are two different ways you can niche. The first is by project. For example, you will see people who operate in a general category as a freelancer, like a graphic designer. But they might choose to only do logos or perhaps create branded PDF books. That's because logos or branded PDF books are very specific projects. This approach is different from the graphic designer who takes on all projects. That person would be called a generalist.

You can also niche by industry. For example, you might work with a particular sector of the industry. And it can be broad, such as working as a virtual assistant in the real estate industry, but then that can get narrower, such as posting real estate listings for international real estate agents.

Now here's the unique thing about these two ways to niche. You can do one or the other, you can do none of the above, or you can do both. I do both. Ninety percent of time I write search engine optimized blogs, which is an example of niching by project. I write them for attorneys and the marketing agencies who help them. I've narrowed my niche on both of those scopes, which helps when I'm marketing my business to new people because then they know exactly what I do, and it telegraphs my level of expertise.

tip

Niching positions you as the expert in your industry, which can help you attract more of your ideal clients.

As I mentioned above, a project or industry niche isn't a must, but it's a good way to scale things down and stay focused during your day to day.

This is because one of the best productivity hacks as a freelance writer is to keep your brain in one lane at any given time. What happens when you ask your brain to do 15 different things during the day? It's exhausting. Your brain experiences fatigue. For example, when you think about people like Mark Zuckerberg and Steve Jobs, they always wear the same clothes every day, right? That's because of decision fatigue.

People in CEO roles and high-level positions within companies have to make massive numbers of decisions and process a tremendous amount of information every day. As a freelancer, you kind of have to do that, too. You have to get to know clients very quickly, decide what's in their best interests, and put your best foot forward and produce an amazing project every single time. Then if you're lucky, you get to continue that relationship with the client. But it can be tiring if you're jumping from one task to another all day long.

Getting More Focused and Productive with Niching

One of the reasons I started niching is because I found that I was moving a lot faster when I was only working on certain types of projects. No matter what type of freelancer you are, if you have clients all over the board, that might appeal to you because there's variety. You never get stuck writing about the same things, and you might even enjoy going from topic to topic. This is a good way to get practice and help you find your niche.

For example, writing about gardening tips, then property division and divorce, then the top five reasons your car might break down can seem chaotic. It's just way too much information to process, and it can make the research and writing process super slow.

In my experience, when I started to niche by project, which meant only writing blogs—no more whitepapers or long-form copy, and only a few emails written for clients—I found myself becoming more productive. I focused on blogs and web content to help attorneys

► My Experience with Niching

When I got started, I took writing and virtual assistant projects on everything. My first painful lesson was from a client who hired me to write software articles and wasn't happy with the final product. It was doubly painful because they were so hard for me to write. It took me days to get one article done, and I didn't enjoy it. The whole time I was second-guessing myself. But I didn't know until I wrote a software article that it was a poor fit for me.

I also spent three years working in a life insurance and annuities brokerage, so I initially started in a financial niche. I figured I'd write about insurance. Since I knew these products well, I thought it was going to be easy. But as I took on a variety of projects, I realized that the life insurance and financial niche was decades behind the content and digital marketing trend. They didn't understand the benefits, so it was a hard sell to get a lot of these clients to realize that not only should they have content on their website but they should be hiring me to do it. That didn't end up being my niche, even though I thought I would be well paid since not everyone would be interested in writing about insurance.

Since I had worked as a legal researcher in college for several attorneys, I thought about legal writing. But I had also quite a bit of experience in education: I was a Ph.D. student, and I had worked as a middle school teacher.

But I didn't know what I didn't know. Working as a freelancer, I didn't know what I would like or didn't. If you are at the beginning of your freelance journey, or even if you are months or years into it, and haven't yet found a niche, that's fine.

I ultimately decided to stick with the legal niche based on my experience working with several clients in that space; they were easy to work with, I didn't have much competition, it was well-paid, the work was interesting, and the clients paid me on time. As you work toward a niche, consider how these elements might influence your choice. I found there wasn't as much demand in the insurance industry for my kind of work, so it made more sense to stick with legal. When I explored education as an option, it wasn't as well-paid and there wasn't demand for consistent work without a lot of pitching on my part, since many of the clients only needed help with one-time projects whereas lawyers needed ongoing content.

rank their websites. That meant that every day when I was writing about different topics, I was still asking my brain to do the same thing.

Almost everything I wrote was 500 to 1,000 words. It was all geared toward the same process. I was working with attorneys all over the country, and they all had the same primary goal and expectations—and that made it a heck of a lot easier for me.

Don't make the mistake of choosing a niche too soon. You don't want to start something and end up hating it. That could be terrible, so you should start as a generalist. You might already be in a position where you've got a variety of different types of projects, and maybe some of your clients are similar but not all of them. But most freelancers begin as a generalist because they don't know what they don't know. You don't know what you're great at yet, and you don't know what may not be a good fit for your skill set.

Your niche really needs to come to you. Don't select a niche for the wrong reasons, like you think it will make you a lot of money, even though you don't like working in it. While a niche is a great way to become a subject matter expert and grow your client base, you need experience first, and that's why working as a generalist is so helpful for new freelance writers.

The Benefits of Working as a Generalist First

When you start as a generalist, it is a great thing because you get experience. You learn what types of clients are out there and how they interact with you, what their needs are, and what it means to market yourself in particular categories and industries.

Here are more benefits of working as a generalist:

- ▶ You learn what types of projects appeal to you based on the work involved.
- ▶ You get more experience and build testimonials from a variety of clients.
- ▶ You record how long certain projects take you from beginning to end to help with pricing in the future.

Getting Your Feet Wet

Sometimes, getting your foot in the freelance door as a generalist has everything to do with the size and type of projects you secure. Being able to really dig into a long project, for example, can let you flex your research muscles and find out what you're capable of. At the same time, getting a few short assignments that you can knock out quickly can free you up for more work in new, diverse topic areas. Certain people prefer bigger projects. Many freelancers love long-term projects like books or writing or overhauling an entire website, which can take months and months, or even years. But sometimes, until you've had that experience, you don't know if you'd hate or love it. This is your opportunity to figure out what you do and don't like.

During these initial projects, or even if you've already had quite a bit of work, you have a great chance to step back and say, "What did I enjoy doing the most?" What projects felt the most seamless? What projects were you passionate about while you were working on them?

It will become obvious to you what you do and don't like. If you've read your hundredth article about the best hip-implant medical devices and you're bored to death and are faking it trying to make it sound exciting, that's a big red flag.

Likewise, you'll have things that you really enjoy. For me, that was blogging. I thought, Wow! I can write these so quickly that my clients can turn around and publish them right away. There are so few revision requests. This is awesome; this is my zone of genius, so I'm going to hang out right here.

> **tip** ⓘ
>
> When you complete projects, keep a log of how you felt when you finished. Was the project tiresome? Did you enjoy the content? What aspects would you change if you could go back in time? If you do this consistently, you'll begin to pick up on patterns that might direct you to your niche.

Collect Samples Early and Often

While you work as a generalist, take this opportunity to build your writing sample portfolio or to ask for testimonials from initial clients. Then use them to launch the rest of your freelance career. If the client allows you to reference your work with them as a sample, add that to your portfolio. Remember that as a ghostwriter most clients will not offer this and will instead prefer to keep your relationship private. This is why your fictional samples are so important because then you are not dependent on clients to allow you use of your completed work.

When you're starting, you might think you don't know how to create these materials, because you don't know what your clients want. But as you get feedback from your clients on projects, you can use that as a template for creating samples.

I didn't know what I was doing when I started either, but I used the feedback from clients in my initial work to tighten my own samples, which helped me land other gigs.

You can also use the feedback as testimonials on your website. Or if it's an Upwork job, you might use the feedback on your profile. And if you're active on LinkedIn, you might ask the client to leave a testimonial on your profile there.

Use this initial work to get your samples created for the niche that you feel yourself gravitating toward. If you think you've discovered a possible niche, you will now have a better understanding of what that niche is and what a finished product looks like, or if you don't produce a product, you'll have an idea of what the client is looking for, and you'll be able to get a great testimonial out of it for the future.

Going from Generalist to Niche Writer

Let's walk through an example of what it looks like to go from a generalist to a niche writer. Let's go almost as narrow as you can, short of saying you only do this for someone in a specific geographic area or for a particular size of business. Perhaps a person starts their freelance career and says, "I like writing, so I think I'm going to be a freelance writer. I also like writing long articles and creating content that sells. I love getting in the zone and producing about 2,000 words. That's really enjoyable. It feels like a good duration for a time commitment. I used to work in a dental office as a hygienist, so is there a way I can niche here?"

Maybe the first couple of projects this freelancer worked on were leaning toward sales copy, which was pitching the teeth whitening services of a particular dentist. While working on these projects, the freelancer realizes "I'm really interested in this. This was a fun project; I really enjoyed doing it, and it paid well."

From there, the writer might decide to offer custom landing pages for dentists. You can see the trajectory of this freelancer: They went from just starting as a writer and taking on a number of different projects to realizing they were good at writing long articles and, finally, to deciding that they were going to write custom landing pages for dentists.

If there's enough ongoing demand for dental landing pages, this freelance writer might choose to brand themselves as the niched expert here. But if there wasn't enough work to provide the kind of income the writer was looking for, they might have to expand their niche at least slightly.

If there isn't enough work in the dental landing page niche, the writer could then focus on writing landing pages in related fields like medicine or health and wellness. Or they could focus on dental writing because there might be more demand for other types of dental copy, like websites, marketing brochures, and email newsletters. While the writer's main interest and favorite type of project is landing pages, choosing to expand that niche slightly might help to secure more long-term work.

There is no push to immediately declare a niche and commit to it. But once you find a niche you're interested in, as long as there's enough demand for it, you can work within it. The only way to know whether there's demand is to start doing research on job boards and pitching clients. This is why most people discover their niche over time because they will have collected enough evidence to know they can get consistent work there.

Reasons to Niche

Now aside from making your life easier, let's talk about the reasons why you'd want to niche:

▶ You get better results for the client because you care about the topic and you have experience in it.

▶ The longer you're in a niche, the more that experience builds on itself, and the better results you produce.

▶ Clients love that they don't have to educate you.

▶ You can claim expert status in an industry or certain project type, making it easier to raise your rates as time goes on and your experience grows.

▶ You focus on only one or two things at a time, decreasing the chances of burnout.

If you're that former dental hygienist who is writing sales copy, and the dentist hires you: 1) the dentist is thrilled that they don't have to learn how to write sales copy or teach you how to do so, either, and 2) they're ecstatic that they don't have to teach you anything about dental health because you already know it. They may give you some tips and pointers, but they're not going to start at square one because you already know the basics. So it's less work on their part because you can be up to speed that much faster.

And over time, in addition to getting better results for the client, you get better and faster at what you do. My speed at working on projects or even understanding and brainstorming things was much slower when I started. I was still learning, and I wasn't sure if these were the types of results that my clients wanted. But over time, I got really fast, and I felt like the final products were getting better and better, too, because I was learning from every experience.

Whatever freelance skillset you have, it's a muscle that you're flexing. The more you flex that muscle and focus on getting better and better, the more naturally it will come to you. You'll know all the tips and tricks. You'll know the tools you can use. You know the common pitfalls to avoid.

All this knowledge allows you to refer to yourself as an expert in that industry. When you claim expert status, potential clients are naturally drawn to you. One of the reasons that certain writers succeed within a well-established niche where they're marketing regularly and getting good results is because they are seen as an expert and a leader.

If you've been doing this for two years, three, five, or ten years, and you've been working on a specific type of project, like a sales copywriter, you're an expert. You know all the top trends, software, and words to use.

When you're an expert, it's a lot easier to convert clients because not only do they not have to educate you but they recognize that you know more than they do, and they're happy to hand off the project to you. Therefore, there is a reduced chance that they're a micromanager. When you have expert status, they're thrilled to just say, "Here are the details. Please do this for us. We don't need to know every fact about how this is being conducted. We trust you. You're the expert."

. And, of course, it's easier to market yourself because you are laser focused on the type of project or the industry. You know exactly who you're talking to.

If you've ever received an email from someone who's selling something, and it feels like they're speaking directly to you, it's because that person has a laser-focused niche. They're talking directly to new moms who are getting ready to have a baby in the next three months, and they know the exact pain points and questions that a person in that position has.

A used car salesman is going to be speaking specifically to someone who is not in the market for a new car and wants to buy used. That buyer wants to get a good deal and a high-quality car as much as they can in the used marketplace. When you work within a niche for some time, you'll become even more experienced about how to reach that target audience, and all this experience comes into play when trying to close prospective clients.

When you know who you're talking to, it's easier to create marketing that feels like those emails you open where it seems like the person is reading your mind because they know exactly what you want and need. So when potential clients come across your website, LinkedIn profile, or Upwork bid, they feel like you're the expert and you're speaking directly to them—and, in fact, you might be the only person who can solve their problems, which is critical.

The Downsides of Niching

Niching is not perfect, and it is not for everyone. If you niche and close yourself off to every possible opportunity, you could miss out on great options. You want to leave the door cracked a little in case something piques your interest.

About a year or a year and a half into my freelancing journey, I was contacted by a recruiter who was working for Upwork and said, "We really think you would be good as a project manager."

I had no training as a project manager (PM), I don't have the certifications, and I was not even completely sure what to do. But she walked me through it and said, "Listen, we have this great well-known company that's looking for a PM. I think you could take your writing skills and make them work as a project manager."

Now if I had completely stayed within my niche and said, "All I really do is write SEO blogs for lawyers. That's all I do, and that's what I'm going to stick with," I would have missed out on the opportunity. My decision to take the Upwork gig led to an assignment working for another company as a project manager, and then for Microsoft as a project manager.

The moral of the story is you can always make exceptions to your niche. If an amazing opportunity comes down the line, and you know you have to try it and think you can succeed, then you want to make sure you have left that door open just a little.

On the other hand, is it going to be the end of the world if you keep that narrow view and miss an opportunity? Probably not, because there's also a chance that if you're well niched, you are fully booked.

Another downside to niching is you could get sick of it. What if you spend all this time establishing a niche, building a website around it, fine-tuning a LinkedIn profile for it, and creating samples that demonstrate your expertise—and then you just get tired of doing it? In this case, you can just start over and choose something different or go back to being a generalist. But it would take some work to go back to that point. You would have to reboot and refresh all your marketing materials.

One common concern is that a niche might get saturated. In most cases, this is unlikely because there are so many clients and freelancers today that there's no way that every client has been served. Just think about how many people run their own businesses or open medical, dental, or legal offices every day. You have more professionals entering the marketplace and plenty of people who are leaving their full-time jobs to pursue their entrepreneurial dream.

There are plenty of clients out there. Even if you target only Fortune 500 companies, you're not going to land a gig with every Fortune 500 company. And even if other freelancers are pitching those major companies, that doesn't mean they're going to land all those great gigs and you're not. The bottom line is there are a lot of options out there, so most niches are not saturated if you have a great value proposition and talent. Ultimately, your writing is likely to be the strongest for topics you're truly passionate about, so this makes niching fun and leads to happy clients.

There can be niches where there's not enough demand, which is something different. If you are an artist who draws comic books that are female-powered, historical manga novels, I don't know if there are enough clients out there for you to rock that niche day in and day out. There could be, but you need to evaluate the demand level first. You can always take a step back, but don't avoid getting into a niche because you think it's saturated. There are lots of opportunities if you're good at what you do.

► Expert Niche Selection Tips

As you select a niche, you should be able to weed out what doesn't work for you and why. Some of those considerations may be deal-breakers. As I stated earlier, one of the top reasons why you shouldn't niche is because you think something will make you a lot of money. If you don't like the topic or the kinds of clients you work with, good money will not even out this experience for you. If you'll be bored the entire time you work on something and it will take you a long time, you'll learn quickly that it is not worth the money, no matter how much the client is paying you.

If you don't have enough experience in a field but assume you can wing it, you are likely mistaken. A company looking to hire an experienced software manual writer will be able to quickly tell that you don't know what you're talking about. Be honest and share that you're new to the field but are a quick study. Or educate yourself on your own. But don't pass yourself off as an expert if you're not. Being a consistent and successful freelancer means positioning yourself as an expert and providing top-quality work all the time.

As you are learning, you'll eventually grow into that expert status, and you'll have lots of you'll have lots of collateral to support your expertise, like testimonials from clients and case studies you can use.

Finally, don't choose a niche just because it appears to be in high demand—especially if it doesn't interest you. For example, if you see there are a lot of talented and high-earning sales copywriters, this alone should not draw you into that niche unless you also love writing sales copy. This can set you up for failure and make for disappointed clients. Consider reading different types of writing examples so you can start narrowing down what type of writing calls to you. For instance, if you love reading sales emails from online entrepreneurs, this could be an avenue for you to pursue. But always make sure you have an underlying interest.

The last reason you shouldn't choose a niche is because you heard from some other person once that it was a good one. That's not a good choice. If someone else is doing well in that niche, that's not a reason for you to launch your freelance career doing the same thing. They may have a different approach, or perhaps they're just lucky and have a big network. Or maybe they've been at this for 25 years, so they know how to sell it. Never choose someone else's niche as your own if you don't have that underlying desire.

Knowing Whether There Is Demand for Your Potential Niche

There are two ways you can research to figure out whether the demand for your niche is there if you haven't looked for it yet. I like to check LinkedIn for job titles and keywords because these listings for full-time jobs are indicators there is a need in a specific field that could be addressed via freelancing.

You'll see recruiter ads on LinkedIn, but you can check out places like Indeed, too, to see what the demand is for the full-time market in your niche. You might see pro-finder posts on LinkedIn as well.. You can see what positions are out there that people have searched for or are looking to hire, which indicates there is some demand. And even if you're not planning to use Upwork as part of your marketing strategy, look for those same keywords on Upwork to see if there is enough demand; are jobs being posted every day for that skillset?

If you're thinking about starting in a certain niche, write a few paragraphs about your experience and interest in this field. Include one paragraph about why you like working in this industry or on these kinds of projects. This step is a precursor to writing a pitch that helps you identify a path toward establishing a unique value proposition.

As a highly niched person, you'll also know all the dos and don'ts, so you'll know where other freelancers fall short and how you can surpass them. You'll also know where most of your potential clients are screwing up because you'll have worked with others on similar projects or in a similar industry. For example, in my niche with attorneys, many of them have the writing skills to create content but not the time. Knowing this ahead of time makes my conversations more effective because it feels as though I'm speaking directly to them when I point out that they are probably too busy to keep up with a blog. And when you own that expert status, your clients will trust you instantly. It makes your sales calls that much easier because you've probably heard most of the questions the client will ask you and will, therefore, already have the answers.

Here's an example of how choosing a niche can benefit you. Let's say you want to write about aging and lifestyle for baby boomers. Your first question is probably "Who can I write for?" You don't need to reinvent the wheel and start from scratch. Think about people or organizations who already serve this segment of the population. You've got retirement professionals, estate planning lawyers, health experts trying to help people stay fit and active as they age, long-term care insurance companies, and organizations like AARP. My point here is there are plenty of companies trying to target the exact type of writing you do because they have a very specific audience. They're already talking to these people and likely need copywriters, too. If you're passionate about marketing to baby boomers, find people who are doing it successfully, and you could help them do it even more effectively. That's an excellent way to make things easier for yourself.

Now that you've got the lay of the niching land and can discern whether going this route is a fit for your skillset and goals, you can focus your energies on securing a strong client base. The best way to do that is learning how to create a great pitch. That's what you will read about in the next chapter.

The Art of Pitching

The only way to connect with your prospective clients is through pitching. It can be a fatal error in your business to assume that clients will come easily, which can sound harsh but is an honest assessment of what it takes to succeed. Your pitch is everything in your freelance business. Simply put, you cannot get off the ground without it. You cannot draw in clients and have conversations if you don't know how to pitch. Most of the time when new writers fail to convert prospective clients or get responses, it's a problem with their pitch. Work samples and pitches sell you to the client, so don't neglect creating and honing either one of these.

Most people who have been working as freelance writers for some time recognize that it can take weeks or months to become good at pitching. Some argue that it takes your first 100 pitches to see what you did wrong and where you can improve. In this chapter, you'll read about the most common pitching mistakes that writers make. We're also going to discuss how to write a good pitch and examples of great pitching ideas. Finally, we're going to walk through some different examples and how pitches might be tweaked depending on the avenue in which you are pitching. Let's start by getting to know the lay of the pitching land with various types of leads.

Defining Warm and Cold Leads

Before we can dive into the mechanics of pitching and walk through some pitching templates, let's talk about the difference between warm and cold leads.

Warm leads are people who don't need to be sold on your service. A great example of where you find warm leads is freelancing sites like Upwork. People on Upwork or similar sites already know they need to outsource that service and have just been unsuccessful in outsourcing it to this point or have past experience outsourcing and want to build on that positive foundation.

Cold leads are those people who have never heard of you or your service. This could be someone who you interacted with on LinkedIn or perhaps a person you met at a networking event, but regardless they might not know that you can outsource this particular task. In these cases, you may have to provide them with some education.

Thinking Like the Person Reading Your Pitch

Do you know that one of the best things you can do as a writer is to think about the reader first? The reader's problems, mindsets, and interests will guide you in the right direction. The same goes for creating a pitch. The more you can think about the person on the other end of your Upwork job post or cold email, the more likely they are to read it and act.

Most people do not spend a lot of time reading a pitch. And they don't have time to review a pitch that is way too long.

This is one of the most frustrating aspects of working as a project manager or as a hiring manager because you have limited time to read the pitch.

▶ Don't Be Afraid to Do Some Recon

When I started freelance pitching, I could not figure out why I was not landing gigs. I thought it was frustrating that all these other people were beating me at the pitching game. They were winning more jobs than me, and I saw myself losing jobs to them on freelance websites.

I decided to game the system and learn from my competition. I created a job on Upwork and invited many writers to respond to it and then looked at their pitches. That wasn't to copy them, but it was to learn what I could do differently.

This exercise helped me figure out my own unique value proposition—what made me different from everyone else. Through my experiment, I saw that some people were beating me on price, something I wasn't willing to drop any lower. Others were beating me on experience. I used that to decide where I could outpace them in either industry experience, speeds, or other bells and whistles I added to my offers, like extra rounds of revisions, free stock photos, or recommendations for future blog titles.

Freelance Project Pitching from a Project Manager's Perspective

As a project manager for freelance writing teams, I have reviewed thousands of freelance writing pitches. And I'd say the failure rate is 60 to 80 percent. As a fellow writer, it pains me to see so many people shoot themselves in the foot with a bad pitch. These writers might not even know that it's their pitch blocking them from getting that foot in the door. I once reviewed more than 200 pitches for a client looking to build a big writing team. We had a high volume of people apply for the jobs to work as virtual assistants or to work as writers, and most of those people did not send a great pitch.

Of those 200-plus pitches, more than 150 were eliminated off the bat. That was unfortunate because a lot of those people might have made a better impression. I didn't even get around to looking at their samples because the pitches were so bad. They spent time putting together their pitch, yet it didn't work for them because they made mistakes—errors that were easily avoidable.

These mistakes depend on the kind of pitch you're sending and the platform you're sending it through, but they generally include:

tip

Treat every gig as if you have ten seconds or less to get the prospect's attention. Doing this, you'll probably tighten up your writing and develop a focused and effective hook, or opener, to your pitch.

▶ Sending a pitch that's too long

▶ Being too focused on your qualifications and not the client's needs

▶ Making generic statements like "I'm a good writer"

▶ Telling a client instead of showing them how your work benefits them or their business

Your best bet is to focus on what your unique value proposition is, how you best fit the job, and what you can create for the potential client. This is discussed further on page 89.

Elements of a Great Pitch

At this point in the chapter you probably want to know what a winning pitch is or how to create a template. There is no standard pitch that will work for all freelance writers. Further, if there was a perfect one, and clients started seeing the same copy and paste from freelancers, they'd write it off as spam.

Great pitches, however, do include several common elements:

▶ An explanation of who you are and your background as a writer

▶ An overview of why you're the right person to help them with their content

▶ Further details about your work, such as links to your portfolio and writing samples

Even though your pitch will be unique for your experience, these elements can lead to a solid pitch every time.

First, start with a great opener. You will lose someone's attention if you cannot capture them immediately with something that is enticing to them. Way too many freelancers kick off with something that's generic. Next, you want to move into showcasing your individual talents—that's your unique value proposition that makes you different from other freelancers.

And, finally, while it might be possible that we could get these prospective clients to hire you immediately, it's far more likely that we are going to prompt them to take some further action, like answering you or accepting your request or opening your samples. All your pitches should have these three elements, and they should be in this order, too.

Starting with element number one, you should have a great opening line or a couple of lines. For the explanation of your background, review your writing resume and think about past experiences with clients. Which examples stand out for you? Which clients did you have the best experience with and who would you love to work with again? Tweak those into your current pitch. Be results-focused when writing these aspects of your pitch, such as:

▶ I have a habit of delivering on time, and it's why most of my clients hire me again.

▶ My clients tell me that my work jumps off the page, and that's my underlying goal in each project I take on.

Even if some of your pitches are a little longer or you have tweaked them a bit and created a template, they should each have all three things in the right order and in the right amount of depth. A couple of paragraphs is more than enough. Remember that your prospective clients are busy and don't care or have time to read a long letter.

A great pitch is all about the client, with bits of your background and talent peppered in. A good pitch should also be unique to you. As a hiring manager, I always gravitate toward freelancers who write thoughtful and personalized pitches. If one freelancer's expertise is their 20 years of experience and you've only been in the field a few months, you wouldn't be able to say the same thing. A great pitch takes your unique value proposition and propels you ahead of all the generic pitches.

> **tip** ⓘ
>
> Develop a pitch, step away from it for a day or two, then come back and review it again. Use this fresh set of eyes to adjust and to fine-tune your words for maximum impact. Don't get too attached to any words or phrases, since you might change these in the future. Your bottom line should be converting clients, and testing your pitch will help you edit and update.

Look for Clues to Pitch Clients

As you craft your pitch and when you have the opportunity, try to read between the lines to figure out what a client wants. You're not going to be able to do this all the time, but you can look for clues.

Especially on freelancing sites or even in a LinkedIn message, a client will tell you exactly what they need and how they might have had a bad experience in the past or share other concerns they have about the process. Any time you can use this type of information to your advantage, it is extremely beneficial to do so.

While you won't always have much information about the client, reviewing their company and asking questions will help you figure out their hesitations. During your phone call with a client, the other person or team is likely to drop clues. For instance, if they tell you that they've worked with a writer before who missed deadlines, this is your chance to talk about your own reliability. Much like how your pitch is focused on the client, this way of learning about your client continues this trend. The client begins to picture what it's like to work with you because you're already positioning yourself as a valuable member of their team before you work together.

When you pick up on one of these clues in a job board post, in an email conversation, or on a phone call, ask further questions if you need more details.

Finding Your Unique Value Proposition

Let's talk a little bit more about you and your unique value proposition, or UVP, which you first read about in Chapter 5. Your UVP is what you and only you can bring to the table. Your UVP matters because it's what sets you apart from everyone else, especially when you are working with warm leads from freelancing sites.

You want to make sure that you are showcasing what makes you different from other people. Your UVP should be woven throughout your pitch so that people know why they should consider working with you and the main benefits of choosing to outsource to a freelancer overall.

If your pitch is missing your UVP or you are talking about someone else's UVP because you copy and pasted somebody else's pitch, it's not going to convert for you because you are attracting ideal clients who are interested in that person's success, not yours.

Here are a variety of UVPs that might apply to writers who are pitching for a gig as a book ghostwriter:

▶ I've written 16 books of my own.

▶ I've been published in *Writer's Digest* and *Business Insider* and know what it takes to get an editor's attention.

▶ My last client increased their sales threefold because of the rewrite I completed of their landing page.

▶ I'm an academic researcher and an expert with projects that require a lot of research.

▶ I've been in this field for ten years and have a firm grasp of industry trends and jargon.

▶ As a former investigative reporter, I can help you write this book by using interviews, transcribing them, and weaving them into a story.

Now do you see why a generic pitch won't work for everyone? Everyone's experience is different. You've got to find what makes you different, too.

tip ⓘ

Ask for feedback from your first couple of clients. Your UVP might be different from what you thought. Usually, your clients will tell you why they liked working with you and what their favorite aspects of your work were. Use this knowledge to land future jobs by including statements in your pitch like "Past clients loved working with me because . . ."

► **Getting the Right Mindset for Pitching**

There are two major purposes for pitching. Where a lot of freelancers fall short is in thinking that the second one is more common. The first is to land a client straight off your pitch, but pitching is not about landing gigs immediately. Getting a client to say yes right away is extremely rare. The second reason to pitch is to begin a conversation that might lead to work.

When it comes to the two outcomes for pitching, both are possible, but more often than not, you are trying to get them to take some other communication action with you. It could be talking to you on the phone. It could be messaging you on freelancing job sites. It could be responding to your email or accepting your LinkedIn connection request.

It's not about getting them to write back to a total stranger and say, "Yes, I want do business with you immediately." It's about using those three crucial elements to a winning pitch you read about on page 84 and making a connection (hopefully a long-term one) with a potential client.

What Do Clients Care About When Reading a Pitch?

Clients care about several different things when reading your pitch. Again, one of them is not reading six paragraphs about you. First, they do want to know enough about you to determine that you are who you say you are.

They simply want to make sure that you're legitimate, you're qualified at whatever type of freelance service you're offering, and you've got the chops to back up the claims you are making. This is where your UVP comes in, which comes right after your good opener.

With your UVP, you're going to have a little bit of lead-in about why you're the right person to do this, then you're going to talk about the proof behind that. That could be testimonials on your LinkedIn profile or special designations, awards, or test results you've achieved. It could also be the feedback on your various professional profiles or links to major publications in which you've been mentioned. There are many different ways to demonstrate your chops. Clients also care that you're a professional and not a fly-by-night provider, which is more common than you might expect.

I'm Done with My Pitch—Now What?

It's never going to be the case that you create one perfect pitch and you never need to worry about it again. Pitching is a numbers game, and you also always need to be refining it.

In the spirit of trying various approaches and refining them, start by storing a general copy of your top two or three pitch drafts on your computer. When it's time to draft a new one, you can copy and paste certain elements of each pitch, then add in unique facets for the client you're contacting. If you previously pitched whitepapers but are now switching to sales copy, you'll want to change the background and experience referenced in the whitepaper pitch.

If you notice that you're no longer getting responses with a certain pitch, it's time to change things out.

Follow the example of entrepreneur, author, and tech investor Tim Ferris, who is known as a guinea pig in the business world because he got his start trying things out, then reporting on the results. As a freelancer, you need to be a Tim Ferris. You will try different formats in your pitch, and based on the results, determine which ones worked best. I learned early on that people did not like my pitches when I presented myself as a company. They responded much better when I was an individual.

I never would have guessed that, but practice taught me to test things and rely on where I had the best results. The same thing happened with the picture I used for my

▶ Track Your Numbers

Once you start pitching clients, keep track of which ones worked best. If shorter pitches had better responses, make shorter pitches your primary focus. Determine what clients liked about your pitch and why your statements stood out.

Using a pitch spreadsheet can keep you accountable and help you to spot trends. If most of your clients are coming from one lead source, you'll use this information to rely more on that lead source. If you notice that many of your prospective clients are dropping out of the sales cycle before you get the chance for a phone call, this data can help you spot the trouble areas and make adjustments.

A pitch spreadsheet with data is powerful because numbers don't lie. If you've set a marketing goal per week or an income goal, your pitch spreadsheet is where the rubber meets the road. If you're doing the work you promised to do, your pitch spreadsheet helps you stay on track and enables you to celebrate goals. Far too often, freelancers get frustrated before they've spent enough time or sent enough pitches. Keep track of your information in a spreadsheet so you can see if you've really sent 50 pitches and had no response, or if it just feels that way. Let your data drive your next decision.

email, LinkedIn profile, and Upwork profile; it needed to be my face and not my company logo. The lesson here is that you should always keep refining your pitch game. Even now, I go back and look at old pitches and try to figure out what makes them a hit or miss. There's always room to tweak things and take a fresh approach. Maybe what worked six months ago or a year ago isn't as effective anymore. This is not a set-it-and-forget-it world. Make sure you remain critical of your pitches, your LinkedIn profile, your samples, and anything else you use to attract and convert clients.

And although it's hard to redo or update things you thought were done, it's helpful to do this because it shows that you are constantly refining and getting better. And as a writer, especially if you are a writer, you need to be updating because you get better and better at your craft.

The pitches that I sent when I launched my business look very different years later. As a writer, you will often notice pitches that could have been written more tightly or writing samples that could have been tweaked and improved a lot more, but you don't know until you get out there and practice. And as you get better and find things in your pitches or writing samples that work, you will update those elements.

Major Pitching Mistakes to Avoid

Now let's talk about some of the biggest pitch mistakes all freelancers are subject to make. These are some of the most common missteps in the freelancing world, so familiarize yourself with them and keep them in the back of your mind as models of what not to do.

A Pitch That's Too Long

The first misstep is making your pitch way too long. Clients are busy. They do not have time to spend 15 minutes reading your pitch.

It does not matter if it's a CEO or a small-business owner, professionals today are extremely pressed for time. And as I shared with you my story of reviewing 200 pitches, clients are not going to go farther than your pitch if it is not stellar.

You are also not impressing your client by throwing everything but the kitchen sink at them. In fact, you are doing a huge no-no, and that is overwhelming your clients. When you overwhelm your clients, they shut down.

People can't make decisions when they are in overwhelmed mode. Have you ever been out shopping and there is a lot going on to distract you? Perhaps one of your kids is screaming and starting to throw a tantrum, the salesperson is trying to explain something to you, and your spouse is calling you on the phone. With all these things are going on, you are not in the best mindset to make a decision. In this situation, usually you just say, "You know what, I can't do this right now, I have to come back."

But when the same thing happens to your clients, like when you say, "Here are ten paragraphs about me and why I am so awesome," your client just shuts down because they feel you are not being respectful of their time and energy by sending them an overload of information. This data dump is overwhelming and comes across as way too much about you. This is the second major pitching mistake, and it's one that most writers make without realizing it.

Talking Too Much About Yourself

Clients are self-oriented people, and they care far more about what you can do for them than learning about you. You are also hiding the best information from them if the greatest details inside your pitch are at the bottom. You want to make sure that your clients can easily find the best possible features about you that will prompt them to take further action. Focusing too much on yourself is all too easy to do when you are trying to come across as credible and qualified. But when you talk too much about yourself, the client doesn't have any reason to act.

To a certain extent, the pitch is all about you. You need to explain your unique value proposition, why the client should hire you, and why your service will make a difference for them. But on the whole, what clients care most about learning is why working with you is beneficial to them, yet so many freelancers miss this.

tip

Even though you want to present yourself as qualified for the gig, always be client-focused. Read your pitch and pretend you were receiving it as a hiring manager. Would it stand out from other pitches? Does it speak to solving the problems of a busy client?

That's the most important part of the pitch. If all you do is talk about how great you are, you are missing out on the opportunity to convert that client. Clients want to know how the blog posts that you will write for them will boost their website's search engine ranking. Or how the brochure that you will write for them will make them money. Or how you taking on their ghostwriting project will make their life easier. That's where clients are motivated to learn more.

Saying "I'm Good at What I Do"

Please do not make this crucial pitch mistake of saying this statement: "I'm a good writer." You'd be surprised how many hundreds of pitches I have seen with some variant on this useless statement.

It is a huge mistake to say this because everyone does it—it's so generic. Of those 200 pitches that I reviewed in my call-for-pitches experiment, so many people wrote "I'm a great writer" or statements like "I've been doing this for five years."

Your client doesn't care; you don't need to prove things that are obvious. If you are a freelancer who is getting paid for your services, it is assumed that you are good at what you do; otherwise, you would have been driven out of business.

Pitching is valuable real estate; do not waste your time on saying something like "I'm really good at what I do. I have been doing this for ten years."

It's a huge mistake to explain that to your clients because they should already know that. And in fact, it takes them back to that point of overwhelm where they don't know what action to take because they start thinking about other people who are possibly pitching them. Why is this freelancer saying they are good at what they do? It's a wasted sentence because it doesn't lead the client to have any sense of urgency, since all they think is that you've wasted their time by making them read that sentence.

Also, if you're pitching on freelance job board sites or anywhere of that ilk, saying, "I'm good at what I do" or "I'm a great writer" doesn't help you stand apart from the competition. It just muddies the waters and goes back to pitch mistake number two of talking way too much about yourself.

At most, you should have two or three sentences about you in your entire pitch. That's it. No more. Not 15 paragraphs about all your credentials, plus a link to your resume and a link to your LinkedIn profile. A couple of sentences on your UVP is enough, then you should dive immediately into why what you do matters for the client.

Expecting an Instant Response

Pitch mistake number four is when you expect an instant response from the client. People will fall off the process at every stage of your pitching. From opening the email and responding to it to scheduling a call and all the way through to a signed contract, the pool of people who will work with you shrinks at each stage.

And here's a harsh truth: The people you pitch to may never respond to you.

The people who respond may never schedule a call with you. The people who schedule a call with you might never go forward with your proposal. There's always going to be some kind of drop-off, so you're not going to get an instant response or hire, particularly if this is a cold lead.

You might not get hired right away. Sometimes people need additional time to review budgets and to look at additional information to decide if details from other freelancers are more compelling or not.

Clients can also easily get overwhelmed if a bunch of different people are submitting pitches and sending in materials. The client will have a lot to read through, and they're going to get overwhelmed and frustrated.

You don't want the client to feel that you're bombarding them with information or pressuring them to make a decision, because at the end of the day they are hiring a stranger on the internet, so you want to provide them with enough details to feel like they can trust you without overwhelming them.

Not Following Up Enough

The final pitch mistake is not following up enough. Just like pitch mistake number four, you can't expect an instant result with pitching. If you pitched one person once, and that's it, no wonder you're not hearing back. It can take dozens of pitches to get a response, and you may have to follow up for a long period of time.

Sometimes they've hired somebody else, or they just get busy and overwhelmed, or they get 25 other proposals and they can't sort through all of them. But if you are pitching cold leads, and you pitch once, then you never follow up, you're not going to hear back.

A lot of clients have a lag and lead time before they can approve whether they want to work with somebody. I've had clients I've had to follow up with for over a year. Now that is not normal or the average, but it shows the value of following up. If you've sent dozens of cold pitches before to people on LinkedIn, cold emails, and social pitches to Facebook groups, but you've never landed any, one of the reasons could be that you didn't follow up.

Pitching is a huge numbers game. It took me 32 pitches to land my first one back when I got started, and it took me years to get to the point where I felt like I had a 30 to 40 percent closing rate, and part of that was in learning how to decide which jobs to bid on. Like I mentioned earlier, you need to be a Tim Ferris and remember to revisit the drawing board on a regular basis.

If something is working, you want to do more of it, but if something is not working, then you want to go back to the drawing board and be able to figure out what is off. What piece of the pitch is missing?

And that's a big reason why it helps to have somebody else look at your pitch and provide you with personal feedback. In the process of being critical of your own work, you're going to learn a lot about yourself and about the way clients think. The more you can start to think like clients, the easier it's going to be for you to write a compelling pitch and to be outstanding on sales calls with prospective clients as well.

If you've submitted 100 pitches and you've received no response, there is something wrong with your pitch, your samples, or both. (Don't question this. Just get help from a pro in reviewing your pitch or samples before you go any further.)

Examples of Great Pitches

As you've read, there is no such thing as the "perfect pitch," though there are certainly some common elements and best practices you can follow. That said, it's also important to recognize when something works well. Let's go over two different types of pitches and discuss why they work and where they might be successful.

Job Board Pitch

Here is a general one that is not tailor-made for Upwork or a similar freelance site. This is a general pitch you might use. Remember, we're looking for those three elements of a good introduction, then your UVP and a prompt for further action:

Confused about creating the right content for your marketing collateral? I get it! Lean on my ten years of experience.

Just reading those two opening sentences gives the client an instant connection about the difficulties of staying on top of content marketing while also positioning the freelancer as an expert.

In the pitch opener, the candidate has done an amazing job of talking about their UVP, which is ten years in business. But they don't stop there. If the freelancer had stopped here, the pitch would be similar to the dreaded "I'm good at what I do."

The next phase of this pitch would be to discuss the freelancer's individual talents and how that ties back to helping the client. The pitch might go something like this:

If you've had some projects on your back burner that you want to finally cross off your to-do list, or you'd like to get ahead on your content marketing, I'm here to help you crush your marketing goals.

Since online content marketing can convert your clients 80 percent more effectively than other methods, I leverage my talent to speak directly to your ideal clients.

I'm free this Friday to chat about how we can get some of those things off your plate. Want to chat?

This pitch is brief, but it also gets the client's interest because it is client, rather than freelancer, specific. The freelancer has put themselves in the client's shoes and closes the pitch with a request to speak further.

This might seem like a minor nuance, but your time to talk about your background is on the phone, not in a long pitch.

Pitch for a New Connection

A general pitch would be most appropriate for someone you've never interacted with, such as a new connection over email or social media. Forging connections on LinkedIn is slightly different.

Connecting on LinkedIn is extremely valuable as a method of growing your business, but it's very different from other types of pitching because it's not going to be like sending in a pitch on Upwork and hoping that the client hires you right away. You might need to nurture a LinkedIn lead for a lot longer than a traditional client, because you have to build that relationship, and the know, like, and trust factor.

Let's look at a slightly different pitch for LinkedIn, then talk about why this one works for this particular platform. You'll learn more about using LinkedIn as a marketing tool in Chapter 8.

Imagine you love writing about pets and pet supplies. Here's a sample pitch based on your passion not just for the industry but for a product you already know and use.

> Hey there! I love what you all are doing over at [Insert Pet Supply Company Name Here]. My dog is pretty much obsessed with his [Insert Pet Supply Company Name Here] bed. Talk about a major problem if it's in the wash (why we now have two!). I noticed your blog hasn't been updated in a couple of months. I wish more dog owners knew about [Insert Pet Supply Company Name Here] because your beds make life easier, whether at home or at the kennel. I'm a copywriter, so everything I do is about connecting your mission and products with the readers who need them. Rockin' email open rates, blogs with high click-through rates, and all that jazz. Anyways, just wanted to say thanks as a raving fan of [Insert Pet Supply Company Name Here].

Did you notice how the prompt to further action is subtle. I'm not asking the client to schedule a call with me or to email me back so we can talk about doing business. It's just about opening that doorway to having a conversation. LinkedIn clients and other cold leads take a while to cultivate.

The chances of a person responding to you from a cold reach-out on LinkedIn and offering you a contract the same day are very low. So instead of our previous pitch example where we were talking to someone who had expressed an interest in having the services of a copywriter, here we're pitching somebody who may or may not need our services. This LinkedIn pitch has more of a personal connection with the client.

We talked about high click-through rates on their blogs and about great email open rates. Those are things that a client would care about. That way, they can see the connection between the copywriter's services that are being pitched and the possible outcome for them.

There's also a lot more personalization in this pitch, which can make it a little challenging if you have a pitch template. However, outside of switching out the name of the company, the bottom paragraph is pretty much reusable, and a lot of the first two sentences are as well. I love what you all are doing over at [Insert Company Here], and then jump into something personal. Maybe it's an article you read from the company CEO, or maybe they were recently profiled in *Vanity Fair* or another magazine. Or maybe it's your own personal connection to the product.

Allowing that to come through is what's been done really well here because the person who opens this connection request or this pitch is going to see that they're not just being pitched services, but they're also receiving feedback from customers, and people want to work with people that they know, like, and trust. They realize that you're already a customer of the pet supply company and you speak highly of their products. That enthusiasm is going to come through in what you write for them.

How to Store and Reference Your Pitch Easily

Once you create a pitch, your next step becomes saving and using it easily. For example, you can create bullet points so you can swap things in and out. Or you can write a strong opening line, then allow for a sentence of personalization.

Once you've created your general pitch concept, then the middle part of the pitch is going to be a little different based on what's being pitched to the client and what you think they might need, but then that last paragraph is going to stay the same. You should then save this pitch and add unique elements to it every time that you send it out.

I like saving a copy of my pitch template in a Google document or on my desktop, so it's easy to jump in and tweak things around. When I'm ready to write a new pitch, I copy and paste my template into a new document and add some additional elements before I submit it on Upwork or send it through LinkedIn.

This makes it easy to get your pitch work done because there are no excuses. You just have to add a couple of sentences of personalization based on who and where you're pitching.

A common question that comes up for a lot of freelancers is "What if I have different services; should I be creating different pitches?"

If you work in a variety of industries and the people you work with are very specific about wanting someone who's experienced in that field, then you should have different pitches for those different industries.

There are several different pitch strategies that you will want to adjust based on where you are pitching and to whom you are pitching. When you're pitching on freelance job boards, the focus is about competition. You need to highlight your UVP and what makes you better than the other freelancers that are possibly competing on this job. You might use some of those general examples I mentioned earlier or the LinkedIn example on page 94 and instead focus on how you can stand out from the competition.

If you are sending a cold pitch, then your focus will be more educational. A client might not have heard of you. Since you have to build the know, like, and trust factor with your client, you should position yourself as a professional and discuss why it matters that they hire someone who is knowledgeable. This educational conversation might include elements of why outsourcing makes sense for this client, why they need the kind of copy you're recommending, and why they should hire you rather than a family member or friend. This is different when pitching on Upwork, which is discussed in Chapter 8, since a client who already knows they need to outsource will be familiar with the basic reasons behind outsourcing.

Finding Clients Online and Offline

It's one of the most common questions asked by new freelance writers and with good reason: "How can I get clients?" Like owning many other kinds of businesses, acquiring customers is completely your responsibility as a freelance writer. If you're uncomfortable putting yourself out there often and likely getting no response or being rejected frequently, freelance writing might not be for you.

As you grow your business, the job of finding clients and trying to convert them to long-term work will remain one of your top responsibilities. This is because when shifting from the employee mindset to the business owner mindset, you have to take charge of creating your own paycheck.

Seeking out and talking to clients is not for the faint of heart. It requires commitment and hearing the word "no" many times. One of the best lessons I have learned is not to take the word "no" personally when pitching prospective clients. It can take time to land clients, and all too often writers are in a hurry to get their first paid gig. But never fall for the myth that it will be easy or that you can snap your fingers and land clients. Successful freelance writers are constantly testing their systems for landing clients and tweaking their approach so they can toss what doesn't work and leverage more of what does.

What follows is an overview of the different ways you can connect with prospective clients. Some will work for you and others might not. That's entirely normal. I have met freelance writers who have built their entire business from landing clients on Twitter, but I have never had a client from that platform. Likewise, I built much of my early freelance writing business on sites like Upwork, but plenty of freelance writers find that it's not the right platform for them.

The key in your business is to keep testing. Track what works and what doesn't. If you can, find a community of like-minded freelancers in which you can ask questions.

Sometimes this advice has helped me try new things. Other times, it's allowed me to close the door on a tactic that wasn't working because I could see from the advice of others that I was going down a path that wasn't helpful. In either case, this is great information to have. Your pitch, samples, marketing strategy, and phone conversation skills all play a role in your marketing process. Don't remain too committed to any one version of these items. I constantly switched up my pitch and my samples until I found a winning combination.

There are methods for finding freelance clients you can use offline as well as online. In general, it helps to have one or two methods you regularly use while you try out a few others. It might take some time to find the right methods for you, but it's never a good idea to rely entirely on only one method of generating business. Let's dive into the offline methods first.

Networking

Networking might seem like an old-school way of generating business, but it can be effective, even in the digital world in which we live. That's because although a great deal of business is done online these days, it can be a lot easier to forge a personal connection with someone when you meet face-to-face.

Networking can occur anywhere in which your client is spending physical time. Chamber of commerce meetings, educational seminars, networking lunches, and conferences are places in which you might connect with your ideal clients. This method of marketing requires a lot of upfront investigation and preparation. It's also dependent on whether your ideal clients are present at these events and, more important, open to hearing pitches.

It's rare to meet someone in person and have that turn into immediate business. It might take a few weeks or months of continued connection with this person to build a relationship or trust. That's why I prefer doing business online, where the customers tend to be slightly savvier about their marketing needs. Distance from a prospective client also rules out the opportunity to meet in person, which can be a time-intensive process.

However, this doesn't mean you should cross networking events off your calendar entirely. Try a few out and determine whether your ideal clients are there. For example, if you love writing copy for dentists, an annual convention of dentists in a nearby area might be worth the trip or sponsoring the conference because so many of your ideal clients will be in the same place at the same time.

In comparison, a chamber of commerce meeting might only have one or two dentists. While one of those could choose to work with you, it's much more effective to choose events or marketing methods in which you have the best chance of reaching as many prospective clients as you can. If you're spending all your time in networking events that aren't giving you a good return on your investment as far as the connections made, re-evaluate and leave them behind.

Direct Mail

Due to the surge in internet marketing, you'll find plenty of people who will tell you that direct mail marketing is dead. But if you're like me, you've probably hired someone because of a postcard or newsletter in your mailbox, so I don't think it's entirely true.

Targeted direct mail can be a powerful way to grow your business. It can also be expensive, which means doing your research about how direct mail works is important if you intend to make an impact. In 2015, the average direct mail conversion rate was just over 7 percent, which means that plenty of people do better than that, but many also do worse.

You can research having your own piece of direct mail created online to get a sense of budget. Setting an

> **tip** ⓘ
>
> Check out Robert Bly's *Direct Mail Handbook* (Entrepreneur Press, 2018) to get the scoop on how to make direct mail work for you.

initial budget of $500 or $1,000, which is usually what you're looking at for a minimum direct mail project, might not be something you can pull off.

As with many marketing efforts in your business, though, direct mail is about what kinds of business you can expect to bring in. If your $1,000 investment yielded several valuable projects, then the initial cost you spent is part of acquiring customers. But I don't recommend dropping thousands of dollars on direct mail until you consider investing in a course or book about it. If you're going to spend the time making use of direct mail, you should leverage all the best knowledge about it and bear in mind that many people will simply throw it away.

A good direct mail campaign introduces what you do and offers the reader some benefit to getting in touch with you right away. Consider what kind of discount or bonus might prompt a total stranger to hire you.

When building a list for direct mail, you can create this yourself or pay a professional to do it. The direct mail list is just as important as the advertisement itself. You might choose to focus on people in your geographic area who don't have a blog as one example. No list will be perfect, but you should carefully curate who you're sending your mail to since you're paying for each piece.

I've also known people who took a direct mail approach to marketing without investing in fancy ads or big lists. They identified ten companies in their area they wanted to work with and wrote personalized letters to those companies. For freelancers I know who pursued this route, the response rate was better, but it's also going to require that upfront work of doing your research and custom writing each letter.

Cold Calling

This is probably a freelancer's least favorite method of doing business, but for that same reason it can be remarkably effective. The rejection you'll experience with any form of marketing is more blunt with cold calling since people can hang up on you or tell you never to call again. However, if you're able to initiate a conversation with an ideal client, all those bad calls can be worth it.

With cold calling, you're going to curate a list of prospective conversations, just like your direct mail list. Here you'll want to make sure you know who you want to talk to at each company. It's likely a marketing director but could also be the company owner.

Have a script ready if you want to cold-call companies. You have a limited time in which to make an impression, so every word matters. You should be offering something that will solve the problems of the person you're speaking to.

Remember that businesses today get a lot of marketing calls and phone solicitation. For that reason, front desk managers are often trained on how to weed out these calls, so know that you have to make it through the gatekeeper before getting to a decision-maker. Most people will have these calls stopped at the front desk or thrown into voicemail, so your cold-calling effort is likely to be more effective if you follow it up with an email or a letter.

Although I love running a freelance business and wouldn't trade it for some other option, that is not to say that freelancing is easy. Constantly refining your pitch process, as mentioned in the previous chapter, can help you stay on the cutting edge.

Direct Emailing

Reaching out to prospective clients over email is another strategy that has been effective for some freelance writers. This is not my preferred strategy of reaching out to people because I have seen that the conversions are much slower and lower when compared with other methods.

But remember, you should always test things out and decide what works for you. There can be some legwork involved in using direct or cold emailing as a marketing approach. One of the most important aspects is that much like direct mail, you will need to cultivate a list of prospective people.

Making a list of brands you would love to do business with or people you know you'd like to forge a personal connection with can be a good first step. Then you'll need to hunt down the email addresses for these companies. You can use tools such as Hunter (hunter.io).

Another resource I recommend installing now if you plan to pursue cold emailing is the HubSpot CRM marketing tool (www.hubspot.com). You will receive a certain number of free email tracking notifications per month that can tell you how many times your email has been opened and at what times it has been opened. This is a great tool for helping you decide who to follow up with. You can, of course, pay for HubSpot's premium version of the service, but I have not found this to be helpful unless I was sending more than 200 emails per month that required tracking.

Cold emailing requires forging a connection with a total stranger in a likely cluttered inbox. This means you need to make a splash and form a personal connection immediately. Sending the same spam message won't work. Consider the differences between these two cold email pitches, both taken from people who were submitting requests to post a guest blog on my website.

Dear Hiring Manager,

I can write about many different topics and am interested in submitting a guest post on your website [insert website here]. Please email me back if you are interested in having me provide this service.

Dear Laura,

I have been following your website for some time and love the various blog posts you have about freelance writing, especially about using Upwork as a tool to generate leads quickly and effectively because the clients are pre-sold on hiring somebody. I'd love to contribute a guest blog post to your website about how to handle a dispute when your Upwork client is upset with your work so that you can salvage your reputation and ideally the relationship. I'd imagine that this piece would be somewhere between 500 to 700 words, but I'm open to your feedback and commentary. I recently went through the experience of going through arbitration on an Upwork job, and I have a couple of key lessons I could share with your audience.

Do you see the obvious differences between these two cold email pitches? In the first example, the prospective guest blog poster has asked me to do all the work. They want me to go look at their experience and to suggest topics for them to write about. They want me to respond and provide further information. In a busy working world, this email is simply deleted. The second email, however, catches my attention because first, the person has taken the time to review my website and to mention some of the materials I've already posted.

They also go above and beyond explaining why they're an ideal fit to write this blog article and how they envision the process going. This makes it much easier for me to tell whether this is a fit and to reply quickly and ask them to submit this blog post to my site.

The same holds true for when you are submitting your freelance writing services. A generic one-size-fits-all approach will not get the attention of your readers.

You are also much more likely to have someone mark your email as spam or to ask to be taken off your list. While you'll certainly get these responses regardless, even with a carefully written pitch, you have a much better chance of a person reading and responding to your email when you use this personalized approach. Also, consider that using your email-tracking tool can give you a significant boost in seeing which versions of your emails are getting the most interest in terms of being opened by prospective clients.

Your initial email in a cold email pitch process is designed to start the conversation. It is very rare and practically impossible that someone will write back with a contract for you to sign and offer you work immediately. You'll need to have a conversation about their needs and write a custom proposal following this conversation.

One of the reasons that I find cold email marketing to be difficult for new freelance writers is that it can take a significant lead time to turnaround such a client. One of my clients that came from cold email marketing required 11 months of follow-up and a few phone conversations before being ready to move forward. For me, this was a long turnaround time and a lot of time invested before I was even paid on the project, which meant that although I enjoyed the work, email marketing is not my top or favorite recommendation for new freelance writers.

You should always test things out though and set a number-based goal for cold email pitching. A lot of experts recommend sending numerous pitches before being effective with a tool like cold email marketing. Your pitching skills will get better and you'll also learn what type of subject lines and pitches work overall from how many people are responding to you or opening your email.

Do You Need a Website?

Most people get in over their head with launching their freelance writing business because they assume they need to invest in building a website before they can start to get noticed by potential clients. I know many successful freelancers, myself included, who do not have a website or did not have one when launching.

Personally, I did not have a website for my freelance writing services for the first three years of operating my company. That's proof that you don't need one. One of the reasons that I do not recommend getting a website too early in the game is that it can be extremely expensive, and far too many people assume that all of the work involved is creating the copy and hiring the right website designer.

A critical mistake people make when using a website as a freelance marketing tool is assuming that "If you build it, they will come." If you do not have a marketing strategy in place to draw clients to your website and attract traffic on a regular basis, it will only be a touch point for people you would have met through other methods anyway.

Leveraging freelance sites and LinkedIn costs much less than putting together a professional website but gives you many of the same benefits. In fact, I felt that sites like Upwork gave me an additional advantage over my competitors who only had freelance writing websites because clients could leave me positive feedback that prospective clients could see.

Building a website can be a way to showcase your work if you do not wish to use job board sites. However, many freelancers still do not need one. With a marketing plan and a place to host your writing samples, such as Dropbox or Google Drive, you can avoid the expense and frustration of building a website. Unless you are a professional website designer who can quickly whip up a site, this will save you a lot of money, headaches, and time at the outset of your freelance writing business.

That time could be better spent creating killer writing samples, a pitch, and a marketing plan. It can cost anywhere from $500 to $10,000 and up to build a professional website. I don't recommend starting your business significantly in debt so if you don't have the money to launch your freelance writing website or the means or knowledge to develop a marketing plan for that website, I recommend you save the money and focus on other marketing efforts.

Set a financial goal for your revenue from your freelance writing business, at which point you might decide to invest in a website. For example, you might decide that after you have earned $5,000 as a freelance writer, you clearly have what it takes to be successful and could benefit from establishing a website. At that point, you would have sufficient income so you would not have go into the hole for too much or too long if you were to build a website.

Elements of a Successful Freelance Writing Website

All that said, if you have the means or ability to create a website and prefer to do so at outset of your freelance writing career, or if you're returning to this chapter after having had some success as a freelance writer and are now ready to invest in building a website, consider hiring a professional or using a hosted and supported website system, such as Squarespace (www.squarespace.com). Squarespace allows you to pay annually or monthly for the hosting and the template on which you can build your website. Taking a quick course over a weekend might enable you to have enough knowledge to build a website on Squarespace, as these templates are easily altered and look quite professional.

The key elements of a freelance writer's website include:

► Links to your samples
► An about you page in which you explain your biography and what makes you qualified to be a freelance writer
► A homepage that directs traffic to the other related pages
► A contact page so prospective clients can reach out to you
► A page for testimonials if you have some
► An explanation of your services page, which might or might not include your pricing

One of the most important things to keep in mind is that your website should be visually appealing and easy for your clients to navigate. Less is more when it comes to adding a menu for your prospective clients. Let's look at some example sites.

Sample Freelance Writing Websites

The homepage for business freelance writer Ana Gotter easily and simply presents exactly what she's all about (see Figure 8–1). The attention-grabbing style of the site, based on simple copy, easy navigation, and colors that are not overwhelming or too bright, highlight her UVP and gives the reader a choice about whether to learn more about her. She's also claiming expert status in her niche as a business writer.

The simple style of her homepage follows throughout the rest of the site, too. You might be tempted to throw everything but the kitchen sink into your website, with text highlighting your background in great detail. However, clients don't have much time, so you need to focus on specifics. Ana's tagline of "expert business writer" clearly explains what she does. For those readers who want to learn more about how she does it, navigating to other pages on the site with similar style means continuity of her concept. Clients will not read thousands of words of you talking about yourself—narrow it down to the top comments. You must be able to grab a viewer's attention immediately. As you can see in Figure 8–1, Ana's focusing on "reach the right audience."

In Figure 8–2 on page 106, you can see the four core services offered by Ana, making it easy—and fast—for a client to determine whether or not to continue exploring her site. If she doesn't offer the kind of writing they need, such as SEO work, the client will likely leave the site. However, these buttons capture attention and focus on her key services clearly.

FIGURE 8–1: **Freelance Website Homepage**

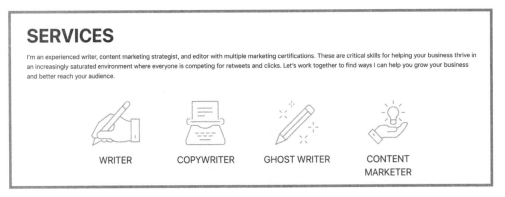

SERVICES

I'm an experienced writer, content marketing strategist, and editor with multiple marketing certifications. These are critical skills for helping your business thrive in an increasingly saturated environment where everyone is competing for retweets and clicks. Let's work together to find ways I can help you grow your business and better reach your audience.

WRITER   COPYWRITER   GHOST WRITER   CONTENT MARKETER

FIGURE 8–2: **Freelance Services Page**

While you're selling a service, never forget that you're selling yourself. Freelance writer Irina Gonzalez has nailed this with her website (see Figure 8–3). On her about me page, she includes a brief bio for clients in a hurry, a photo of herself, and an extended bio for those who want further details.

As you can see, Irina has included links to her work to make it simple for clients to check out her samples and style. Her picture shows her personality and helps to forge a human connection.

Where possible, make your samples into clickable links or images. You can see an example from my own site in Figure 8–4 on page 107.

These are just a few examples of important elements you can and should include on your freelance writing website. Speaking of important elements, let's also talk briefly about whether you should include pricing.

About Irina

Irina Gonzalez is a journalist, writer, and editor based in southwest Florida, covering Latinx culture, sober living, parenting, and all things lifestyle. Her work has been featured in *Oprah* magazine, *Glamour, Marie Claire*, and more. She's also the founder of the Self-Care For Writers newsletter. When she's not working, she is probably reading an audiobook or cuddling with her husband and their attention-loving kitties and pup.

Want to get in touch? Email Irina.

Extended Bio

Irina Gonzalez is a journalist, writer, and editor with over 14 years of experience in digital women's lifestyle publications, including *Latina* magazine, SheKnows, *Family Circle*, MamásLatinas from Cafe Mom, Brit+Co, Blavity's 21Ninety and more.

She is the Managing Editor at The Temper — which explores life through the lens of sobriety, addiction, and recovery with an unapologetically intersectional feminist approach — and a freelance writer covering Latinx culture, sober living, parenting, and all things lifestyle. She has written for *Oprah* magazine, *Glamour, Marie Claire*, VICE, HuffPost, *Women's Health*, Healthline, INSIDER, The Kitchn, them., Ravishly, Eat This Not That, *Good Housekeeping* and more.

Hello! I'm **Irina Gonzalez**, a journalist, writer, and editor based in SW Florida.

I'm the Managing Editor at The Temper — which explores life through the lens of sobriety, addiction, and recovery with an unapologetically intersectional feminist approach — and a freelance writer covering Latinx

FIGURE 8–3: **Freelance Website About Page**

FIGURE 8–4: **Clickable Links**

Including Pricing on Your Website

Freelancers have differing opinions about whether you should list your pricing on your website. Some feel that this turns off prospective clients who don't realize that your rates might be negotiable or that they are based on a specific type of project. On the other hand, some freelancers will argue that listing your pricing helps you avoid unnecessary emails from people who can't afford you.

You might choose to list your pricing item by item, to not list rates at all, or to fall somewhere in the middle by explaining that your quotes start at a certain number based on the project's requirements. That is ultimately up to you, and as with other things in your freelance business, it's helpful to test different scenarios and see what's most effective.

Testimonials on Your Website

Although you're new to the freelance world, make sure to ask for testimonials from your first couple of clients if the projects go well. Testimonials from past clients are excellent social proof. Even if you're a ghostwriter, you can ask your clients if you can use generic terms for their business, but their actual words. For a long time, I was unable to use quotes with the name of the client because of the disclosure agreements I signed with them. But over time, I'd always ask my clients if they were willing to provide me a testimonial just in case. I keep a saved copy of all my positive feedback from clients in a document in case I ever want to send it directly to a client or update my website or LinkedIn profile. For more examples of testimonials, including some that do not name the client directly, please see http://www.legalseowriter.com/testimonials.

Creating a Marketing Plan for Your Website

Your website is an additional space to store your work samples, to explain more about your process, and to connect with prospective clients, but unless you are engaged in some type of marketing plan, your website will just sit there and the only clients who will discover it will be the ones who found out about you through another way, such as a reference from another client that leads them to Google you or to visit your site outright.

A marketing plan for your website could include:

▶ Generating paid traffic using tools such as Google or Facebook ads
▶ Writing regular blog posts on your site and ensuring that you have appropriately optimized your website for search engines
▶ Appearing on podcasts and referencing your website at the end as a place where people can visit and connect with you
▶ Using your business cards to direct traffic to your site

It can take a long time to generate traffic on your website so make sure your site is a tool you can regularly use and is worth the time and money invested. My primary marketing tool on my website has been writing search engine optimized content that I also share across LinkedIn. This has helped generate more cold traffic to my website and makes it worth it to pay the annual fees to have it hosted on Squarespace. If you are not an expert in search engine optimization, however, you might prefer to keep your website relatively basic as if it were only an online portfolio.

When creating your website, make sure to write copy and consider design elements that speak to your end reader. What you might like on your end might not speak to your ideal client and could even lead them to bounce off the site faster than you expected. Putting in the effort to discover design elements that make it easy for your website to be navigated and friendly in terms of the color schemes makes a big difference in whether people decide to stay on the site.

As I said earlier, many new freelancers are under the impression that if they do not have a website, they will not appear professional. Rest assured, I know plenty of freelancers who still do not have a website for their writing services and have been able to leverage other means to grow their company effectively.

Do I Need a Professional Email Address?

This is another area of concern for freelancers just beginning to launch their business. You might want to establish a website because it will give you a professional domain name on which you can establish an email address.

While this will help to make your email look more professional, it is not a necessity. This doesn't mean I recommend having an email address that is unprofessional, such as ilovecats123@gmail.com, but your name or your business's name @gmail.com or at another provider can still be viewed as professional.

In fact, sometimes spam filters are very mindful of an email address that includes a domain name and appears to be an unsolicited pitch. If you intend to use cold email marketing methods to grow your business, be aware that you might have more success with yourname@gmail.com instead of yourname@yourbusinessdomain.com.

Test it out and see what works best for you, but there's no need to invest in a professional domain-managed email address until you are committed to this as a side hustle or a freelance career.

Google Domains and G Suite are excellent and affordable tools for freelancers who want to have a professional email address. Starting at just $5 a month, you'll get all the benefits of Google's standard suite of apps, plus a custom business email address and more. This can be an easy way to get launched quickly without having too many expenses or costs. Google Domains, much like GoDaddy, NameCheap, and Just Host, allows you to purchase a domain name.

Understanding Hosting

If you don't use Squarespace or another website to take care of the hosting for you, you will need to purchase a domain name, hosting, and a platform or template on which the site will be hosted. WordPress (www.wordpress.com) is a popular choice for those who decide to go it alone. Hosting simply means purchasing storage for you to add material, like content or photos, to the site. Many built-in free website builders come with very limited storage. A turnkey solution like Squarespace takes care of the hosting for you. They have different plans available depending on how many subpages you need. Since most writers only need limited storage space and several subpages, this is a big reason why Squarespace is often used. As an all-in-one solution, you can pay monthly or annually for Squarespace to get pre-made templates to build your site on. The downside is that customization is harder than on WordPress, but few writers want or need the customization that would be required with other businesses.

WordPress is relatively easy to use, but it can be just complicated enough that it makes sense to retain a

tip

If you're hesitant to invest in a comprehensive website, purchasing a domain and professional email address through Google still helps you appear professional.

professional to install it on your website. If you do not go with a fully hosted option, such as Wix or Squarespace, you must either retain a hosting service or purchase enough storage space to build and host your own website. Wix is another option but one that still requires some level of web design knowledge. Many Wix sites are easily spotted as a site built on Wix unless you engage the services of an outside designer.

Other hosting services to consider are JustHost and BlueHost. There are many great tutorials online to help you connect these to your WordPress or Wix site, or you can hire a professional from Upwork to help you.

WordPress has a great SEO plugin known as Yoast (www.yoast.com). Yoast allows you to see how much the individual page you're working on has been optimized for search engines, which can be helpful if you intend to use that as a primary method of marketing your website.

A Note About Domain Names

Do some research to determine what domain names are available. In my experience, my name was not available, so I created a website with my company's name instead. Domain names can often be purchased very inexpensively, especially if keep an eye out for sales. Domain names can cost anywhere from $10 to $30 a year.

Some of the various providers that will help you with domain name purchases include:

▶ GoDaddy (www.godaddy.com)
▶ Namecheap (www.namecheap.com)
▶ Squarespace (www.squarespace.com)

Note that if you purchase an annual plan on Squarespace, they will also provide you with a domain name; however, if you do not buy an annual plan, you can still get a domain name for an additional fee.

> **tip** ⓘ
>
> To drive traffic to your website, I recommend writing content with search engine optimization (SEO) in mind and posting a blog on your site at least once per week. The blogs on your site should be driven by SEO keywords and cross-posted in other locations, such as social media.

A Note About Proper Keyword Strategy for Your Website

Recommended keyword density or the amount of times in which your keywords should appear on each individual page is somewhere between 2 and 3 percent. This means that you will mention the keywords several times throughout the course of a 500- or a 1,000-word piece. If you are using WordPress and have installed the Yoast plugin, Yoast can tell you whether you've used your keywords enough.

Supplementary keywords should also be used throughout. For example, if you are a health-care writer, you might craft a blog around the primary term, *medical writer*. But you might also use supplementary terms, such as *freelance medical writer* or *medical copywriter*. These won't be referenced as frequently as the primary keyword, but they can still be helpful for sending a message to the search engines about what your content is about.

Ultimately, keywords are your way to signal to search engines what the primary topics are on your website and a particular page of your site, which can help you rank for those keywords when people enter search terms in Google. Using this as a strategy has helped drive traffic to my website and receive requests for information and quotes directly through email. This is why the contact page of your website is so important. You want to have a way for your prospective clients to get in touch with you.

Connecting with Prospective Freelance Writing Clients on LinkedIn

Most people have the impression that LinkedIn is a somewhat stale social media website, but that has changed in recent years. In fact, LinkedIn is one of the most powerful tools in a freelance writer's arsenal because many of your prospective clients choose LinkedIn as the social media platform on which they are the most active. Understanding this can help you leverage the power of instant connections and getting your pitch and work samples directly in front of people who are making critical decisions about content marketing.

LinkedIn helps break down the barriers between you and potential clients, making them just a connection or conversation away. Furthermore, many people recognize that LinkedIn is the social media platform of choice for business professionals and might be more open to responding to a message on LinkedIn or interacting with you there than through an email or a phone call.

Another powerful aspect of using LinkedIn has to do with the fact that people are using it as a recruiting tool for full-time positions and contract work on a regular basis.

In 2018 I landed more than $35,000 worth of annual work from my LinkedIn profile being properly optimized and regularly posting articles directly relevant to my target client audience. This is because recruiters and clients are regularly searching for keyword terms that you can use in your profile to help you stand out.

This makes it much easier to generate conversations since clients might seek you out, but LinkedIn's opportunities are not limited to this form of passive marketing alone.

Being active on LinkedIn as a marketer, and forming connections, participating in groups, monitoring your own group, and more can all help you to grow connections and have a warm pipeline of leads at the ready at any time.

Unless you are someone leveraging LinkedIn in an extreme fashion to grow your leads very quickly, you probably don't even need to pay for the premium service on LinkedIn. This means that when used properly, your only investment in LinkedIn as a lead generation tool is the time that you spend writing your connections and identifying top contacts.

There are many advanced sales strategies for using LinkedIn to generate freelance writing business for you. Some of the most important things to keep in mind with your LinkedIn profile include:

> **tip**
>
> Use LinkedIn as your professional profile and portfolio if you don't want a website or don't have the time or money to invest in one. LinkedIn is easily searchable and shows whether you're open to connections from possible clients and recruiters.

- ▶ Writing a tagline of what you do and who you do it for
- ▶ Including all the services you offer clients in the overview section of your profile
- ▶ Pulling your LinkedIn connections list to ensure that you are only connected with your ideal clients such as C-suite executives, marketing professionals, digital agency owners, and CEOs

Also keep in mind that using LinkedIn as a lead-generation tool does not give you carte blanche to spam people. If you've been active on LinkedIn for any period, you've probably received these spam-like messages yourself and, if you're like me, completely ignored them. Make sure that you're always presenting value when connecting with a prospective customer, whether it's just to request that initial connection or to suggest having a phone call together to discuss their copywriting needs.

Today's business professionals are overloaded with information, and you must have a clear value proposition to make the connection seem worth it. Personalize your request, such as mentioning something you have in common, perhaps a place you went to school together, or reference some piece of their brand or content marketing that drew your attention.

This is a great way to show that you are not sending mass spam messages to hundreds of people on LinkedIn and are instead targeting ideal clients directly. This form of personal conversation is much more likely to be opened and responded to.

There is so much you can do with LinkedIn. Check out the resource section of this book or the *Ultimate Guide to LinkedIn for Business, Third Edition,* by Ted Prodromou (Entrepreneur Press, 2019) to get more tips for using LinkedIn as a freelance writing lead-generation tool.

Using People You Already Know to Grow Your Freelance Writing Business

You may already have people in your immediate circle who would like to work with you or could refer you to others. Bear in mind the advice shared elsewhere in this book about working for friends and family.

However, if you are truly stuck, getting your first couple of gigs from friends and family who already know, like, and trust you, can make breaking into the world of freelance writing easier. Start with telling your existing field of connections about your decision to launch a freelance writing business. This includes a post on LinkedIn and your personal Facebook page if you have a lot of prospective connections who might hire you for the type of writing you like to do. This can be an easy way to generate your first couple of jobs.

Here is an example of a post you might share on social media if you have recently decided to break in doing resume editing:

> *Hi friends! I just realized today that some of you might not know that I have launched a freelance resume writing and editing business. I have been helping people behind the scenes to land those all-important job interviews and to make an impression in 20 seconds or less. If you need a resume reboot, I am currently offering a special for friends and family. Whether you are just starting your job hunt or are looking for a way to make a splash with prospective human resource managers who may be hiring, I have about five spots open on my calendar for this next week. Leave a message below if you need some help sprucing up your resume.*

This simple, candid message breaks the news that you have decided to launch a freelance writing business, focusing on resume editing, and it can help you get your first couple of gigs. Even if you charge the low sum of $20 or $30 to edit these first couple of resumes, you'll have secured your first couple of clients and made a return on your investment in this book. Furthermore, you never know who your third-party connections are. This means that you might have people in your network who know others who are looking for freelance writers or who could benefit from the services you offer. Having this additional layer of connection and referral can help you land a gig that you might not otherwise have known existed.

I have seen freelance writers use this technique to launch their business as well as to pad their income during an otherwise dry spell. You can tweak your offerings and the discount offered based on the time of year and what you choose to focus on. For example, I know a freelance writer who used this to generate extra income by offering to rewrite people's existing about or bio pages on their website.

She completed three of these over the course of a week and made extra income while getting some additional testimonials and adding some new prospective clients and connections to her roster. Think about your individual writing interest. This can also be an opportunity to try out a new form of freelance writing that you are thinking about delving into without committing 100 percent. If you only take on a couple of freelance clients and edit their resumes, then discover that you hate it, you are not obligated to take on any future clients, but you'll still have the experience, income, and general testimonials.

If you are considering trying out a new service, unveiling it at a beta price and enabling a couple of people to opt in early to test whether you like it and have the skillset for it can make either entering the service or deciding not to offer the service much easier.

Using Freelance Job Board Sites

There are numerous freelance-specific job sites out there, such as Guru, Freelancer, and Upwork. They each have different rules and types of projects posted, so you might choose to cast a wide net and review them all before committing. Other freelance job boards, like ProBlogger, are a way to connect with prospective clients but are not the same as a third-party service like Upwork. These third-party services require that you become a member of their platform and get paid through their platform. Other websites like ProBlogger or Writer's Weekly post gigs with the contact information attached should you decide to pitch a particular client on your own. These websites can be more competitive since your pitch will likely go up against experienced writers.

Among the freelance community, you will find a variety of opinions about using freelance job board sites. Freelance job board sites might not work for you at all. You will find that your personal experience will vary. There are some people who swear by certain freelance job boards and others who argue that they are never worth your time. Having landed substantial long-term clients as well as one-time $50,000 and $25,000 projects on sites like Upwork, I find they can be a valuable lead source, but that requires learning the platform and working hard on your pitch and samples.

Job board sites allow you to interact with clients who are already pre-sold on purchasing your services. The reason I can recommend freelance job board sites is that the clients have already taken the effort to write up specifics about their job proposals. At the minimum, it's worth your time to scan the job boards each morning when you launch your business to see what's in demand and whether there's anything worth bidding on.

Clients visit these websites, share job proposals with the specifics of what they hope to accomplish, then ask for quotes as far as a rate and timeline from interested freelancers.

Upwork is the world's largest freelance job board site, but as I mentioned before, there are mixed opinions about its use. There are many different freelance job board sites out there, and you'll find success stories and complaints about each one. Give each one a fair shot before making a final decision.

Freelance job sites are not appropriate venues for everyone, as it, of course, depends on market demand. Before even signing up, you should evaluate the site and determine whether it is appropriate for you by seeing if there are enough jobs posted in your ideal category and type of project. Bear in mind that many people who post a job have a basic idea that they intend to outsource the project and hire a freelancer, but that the budget notations on these projects can be inaccurate.

The ability to establish feedback and to grow yourself in a community can also be beneficial, but it can be difficult for people to break in. I will also note that there are numerous categories for freelancers posted on the Upwork website, and writing tends to be one of the most competitive.

tip

Don't get hung up on one method as "the only way" for you to grow your business. Writers will find success in different places, so be open to testing ideas and tracking what works. Do method-specific research to make sure you're approaching each option in the right way, since this could require a new strategy or pitch style for each one.

Rate-Setting Tips

Deciding who to work with and how to price yourself are both key elements of launching your freelance writing business. In this chapter, you'll learn how to set rates and adjust them based on your experience creating samples and working on your first couple of projects. Creating your samples is a great opportunity to see how long it takes you to complete projects of different sizes, so keep that in mind as you get ready to set rates.

How to Determine Your Initial Rates

One of the easiest ways to determine your rates for freelance writing projects is to do research and see what is already out there in the market. This information can be helpful to a point, but you will also find that there is a dramatic range, which can lead to further confusion.

You will find people who charge the bottom end of the spectrum and are comfortable making that amount of money, all the way up to the people who have a smaller client pool because of their expensive rates but still enjoy their work as a freelance writer and are able to find enough of it to book them full time.

Both considerations can be helpful when designing your own rates. Getting information about freelance writing rates can begin by thinking about your overall experience and knowledge of the market.

A new freelance writer is unlikely to charge as much as someone who has been working at this for two, five, or even ten years because the experienced freelance writer has likely increased their skills with certifications, trainings, and, of course, the knowledge gained from working with numerous clients.

Different factors will influence your rates, including:

▶ Your experience in the field or the writing world
▶ The technical expertise or amount of research required for the project
▶ The estimated time to complete the project
▶ Whether other aspects of your time, like conducting interviews, will be part of the project
▶ The length of the project

At any experience level, you will find writers charging rates along the spectrum, so there is no one-size-fits-all "rate" to charge.

How Most Writers Charge

How a writer charges depends entirely on their preference, the industry, and the client's willingness to accept that rate. Most writers start their career online with hourly rates, since this is the easiest way to determine what to charge. Few writers charge per page, although that method of pricing is common for editors. Many writers charge per word or per article.

Clients tend to prefer upfront pricing in terms of a per-word rate with an agreed maximum length or a flat fee based on the writer's quote. Included below is a sample, but this by no means an industry rate you should or have to use. It's one example of how to convert a per-word rate to a flat fee per article.

If a client asked you to create a 1,000-word article and you'd usually charge 20 cents per word, this can easily be converted to a $200 flat fee (1,000 x .20 = $200). If you agree to a flat fee, you would not charge an additional rate for extra words added. Instead, you'd usually say that the article will be at least 1,000 words. You'll find writers who charge by the word across the spectrum—some charging five cents as beginners and more advanced writers charging $1 per word. I don't recommend starting any lower than ten cents as a beginner and raising this until you find your sweet spot. The above example references a writer who charges 20 cents per word, but this does not mean that's what you have to charge.

Hourly rates are tricky in freelance writing. Most nonwriters have no concept of how long it takes to write something. That means clients are hesitant about hiring someone who appears "too slow" even if the time involved is perfectly reasonable. This process also means that fast writers get penalized for working quickly. Instead, an hourly rate is a good starting point for creating an estimate, but it's not something most professional writers rely on over the long run. If you're not sure how long a project will take, however, then giving an hourly rate range is a good place to start with your first couple of clients. In general, it's easier to convert clients into paying flat fees for the completed piece unless you're clear up front about how many hours you expect the piece to take. No client likes to receive an invoice with far more hours than anticipated after the fact.

Researching the Market to Determine Demand

A great place to research and find averages in the market is Upwork.com. As I said earlier, Upwork is quite controversial in the freelance world, although it has been essential for helping me to build and grow my freelance writing business. Upwork can give you a better sense of what types of clients and freelancers are out there and what they are charging.

Like I did when researching other writer's pitches, I recommend setting up a job on a freelancing website, with no intention of hiring anyone, and asking for freelance writers to submit their information.

tip

Explore the profiles of the most successful Upwork freelancer profiles in your niche or industry.

On Upwork, you can also research popular freelance writers in various categories and often see what they charge by looking at their work history.

This information is a good starting point when trying to develop your own rates. It can be difficult to figure out how much to charge per project, particularly if you are leaning toward applying a fixed rate rather than an hourly one. Coming up with an hourly rate you are comfortable with is the first step in the process.

Estimating the Time Needed Before Creating Your Rate

Estimating how long it will take you to complete a project is the next thing to consider when developing a fixed rate. Your estimate might not be perfect, but it's a good idea to use your own experience of creating your writing samples to determine what your fixed rate might be. Your fixed rate should include all elements of creating the writing piece itself, from research and writing to editing and submission. Many clients will also want at least one round of revisions, so ensure that you have added that in as well.

Your base rate is the hourly rate you are comfortable with—which you believe the market will bear—calculated by the number of hours you think it might take you to complete the project.

There are other special considerations to factor in, such as extra elements your clients might want you to add. For example, if you're doing SEO writing, a client might request that you include SEO keywords and links to other pages on their website. A person writing a whitepaper will need to factor in interviews with important stakeholders and accommodate for this in their rate. If a client asks you for other elements, such as posting the article to their website, distributing it on a press release service, adding in photos, or more, this can increase your overall price.

Once you have your baseline price, you have a number to begin working with, although you might not always charge this rate. Each project will be different, and you might also wish to reward clients who are hiring you for multiple projects or who are putting you on retainer.

Another important element to consider is what you intend to accomplish with your freelance writing business. If you are simply looking to grow a side hustle and add additional income, then your hourly rate might not be as important to you as someone who is attempting to replace their full-time job.

This online calculator (https://www.calculators.org/savings/wage-conversion.php) will help you determine your financial goal and the hourly rate you need to charge to achieve it, assuming you work a certain number of hours per week.

Remember that not every hour you will be working is a billable one, because you will be spending a lot of time marketing to clients as well as time doing administrative tasks, such as submitting invoices. Further, you probably won't work every week of the year since you'll want some sick time and vacation days, so adjust your rate accordingly.

Getting Paid as a Freelance Writer

There are two primary ways you can get paid by a client: hourly or a flat fee per project.

The most common type of project when you are first starting your freelance writing business is a one-time project or one-time fee. This means that a client will contact you to ask how much you would charge to write one piece of content. You would come up with the amount of money that you deem appropriate for that project and send it back to them as an estimate.

The terms of how this one-time fee is to be paid is up to you. If possible, get some of this fee up front as a sign of good faith that the client will pay you. Far too many freelance writers have been burned by waiting until the content has been approved before they ask for their full payment. If

> **tip**
>
> Most clients understand that asking for a down payment is a good way to start the relationship and show good faith on their part. Don't be afraid to ask for a deposit on bigger projects.

▶ Relying on a Retainer

When working with clients on a retainer, you might have shifted your hourly or flat fee over to a monthly maintenance amount or a contract that you charge within the scope of a particular set of parameters every month. Retainers operate somewhat differently from flat-fee and hourly jobs, in that you might give your client a slight discount in exchange for them signing a longer contract to work with you.

Retainers are a valuable tool for a freelancer, since you can better predict your income and know how much marketing work you need to do to bring on other clients. There are many different types of retainers, most of which are for advanced freelance writers handling numerous long-term clients at a time. It can be hard to convert new clients into retainer clients on your first few projects, so focus on landing clients and delivering high-quality work to start with. Over time, retainers are a great option for expansion.

you do not have some sort of protection worked into your contract or an ability to pursue accounts payable when someone has neglected to pay you, waiting until the end of the project can be a big mistake.

For this reason, most freelance writers will charge 25 or 50 percent of the total project cost as an advance or deposit. There are situations in which this deposit amount does not make sense, such as if the project is very small, like $50.

Using Milestones in Your Contracts

In some situations, it may be appropriate to consider accepting payment at the conclusion of the project. But any project that is larger or includes any amount over several hundred dollars should have defined payment parameters. I recommend breaking these projects into milestones, even if you are not working on an hourly basis. A one-time project can be broken into numerous milestones at which point you will be paid for each submission. An example of breaking a project into milestones includes consideration of the depth of the project and the steps involved. Let's consider writing five blogs for a client.

The milestones might look like:

▶ Milestone 1: Submission of all five blog topic ideas for approval by the client.

▶ Milestone 2: Submission of the first article and requested revisions made by the client.

▶ Milestone 3: Submission of two additional articles, pending final revisions by the client.

▶ Milestone 4: Submission of remaining articles, pending revisions by the client.

▶ Milestone 5: Final payment to be released after all content has been approved following revisions.

Breaking even one-time projects into these smaller milestones provides clarity on the deadlines required and when a client owes you money. It is much easier to determine whether someone can pay you the money when you break a project into milestone amounts because if they skip the first payment, you are not obligated to complete the remainder of the project.

This is a great way to show that you are a professional and to ensure that you have protected yourself as much as possible. Most people prefer to work on a one-time project fee or a per-project basis because of numerous concerns that the clients have around charging hourly.

There are some cases, however, when it makes more sense to charge the client on an hourly basis, particularly if you are not exactly sure how long it will take you to complete a project. Clients tend to be hesitant about working on an hourly basis unless it is absolutely required. You will often find other types of freelancers, such as project managers or virtual assistants, working on an hourly basis, because it can be difficult for them to chart out a per-project price.

That being said, writing often works better on a one-time project or per-project basis, because clients do not want to pay you for working eight hours on a project that should have taken only four.

> **tip** ⓘ
>
> Where possible, convert hourly projects into flat fees once you know about how long and how much work it would take for you to complete the project successfully.

Furthermore, consider working on a per-project basis because you should not be penalized for working quickly. A client who assumes that you can write six 500-word articles over the course of an hour will attempt to pinch every penny out of you and try to make you take a lower hourly rate. This means that you do not get paid appropriately because in many cases it will take you much longer than this considering the research, writing, editing, and submission process.

Creating Rates and Quotes Based on the Whole Writing Process

Writing often requires consideration of every element involved in the project, and it is better for you to approach a project with the idea of getting paid per piece, rather than per hour. Clients do not like receiving invoices for items they did not expect, which is why it is a good idea to discuss up front how long you think it will take you to complete the project and the overall fee.

Even when it appears obvious to you, it is helpful to remind your clients exactly what is and is not included in your fee. One excellent example of this has to do with revisions. The client might have the expectation that they will get three rounds of revisions. But if the project fee you quoted only includes one round of revisions, it's a good idea to state this up front during the process of creating your estimate as well as in your contract so the client knows when they have exceeded the agreed-upon quote. This is what makes contracts so important, because you may need to refer to this information. Including these details in your project quote helps clarify when the client is attempting to push the boundaries.

Hourly Projects

Hourly projects are most often suited to copyeditors or proofreaders who might be doing this type of work, in addition to or alongside working as a writer.

It can be hard to tell when you launch your freelance writing business how long it will take you to complete a project, and many freelance writers start out charging hourly because of this. But once you're established, avoid charging an hourly rate. Eventually, you will get faster at completing your writing, and you should not be penalized for working quickly. In addition, you will always have to carry out the process of choosing topics, drafting pieces, getting client feedback, and incorporating it.

Because clients have no concept of how many hours it will take you to complete a project, it's far easier, as discussed previously, to take an hourly rate and convert it into a per-project rate. For example, say you agree to complete a writing project for $50 an hour. Clients tend to be wary of open-ended hourly projects to begin with, but you can easily convert this to a $200 flat project rate if you anticipate that it will take you approximately four hours to complete it ($50 x 4 hours = $200).

Charging a flat rate will avoid any misunderstandings and surprises on your client's bill. And because many client relationships fall apart due this lack of understanding, this is a good practice to start.

The only downside to quoting a project like this, whether it's hourly or on a per-project basis, is that if you undercut yourself, you cannot go back to the client and say that that you underestimated the hours involved and that they now owe you more money.

The best way to determine what you should charge when converting an hourly project to a flat project rate comes only with some practice. You can make a good estimate based on the information provided to you by the client and additional questions that you ask them, but ultimately you are responsible for determining what to charge. Hourly projects tend to be more appropriate for those jobs where you need to go back and forth quite a bit and for which it is impossible for you to figure out how long the project might take. For example, if I am building a landing page for a client, I might have to do a phone call with them, transcribe the notes of that call and write up my own notes, create an outline, get that approved, get on another phone call with the client, and then email back and forth revisions notes. This means that it's hard for me to estimate how much time upfront I'll need to spend in communication with the client. Hourly rates ensure you get compensated for all this extra nonwriting time that is still part of the project.

Taking on a job as a freelance editor, which is a common side hustle or additional service offered by freelancer writers, makes it difficult to charge per word or per project. Although some copyeditors and proofreaders do charge per word or per project, they can quickly get in over their heads because there is a vast difference between someone who wants minor polishing on a project and a project that has not been written by a native English speaker and may require comprehensive edits. This is why it is a good idea to ask for a sample of the writing before quoting.

Many freelance copyeditors and proofreaders prefer to work on an hourly basis because it means that they are only paid for the time spent working on the project. If you charge hourly, you are responsible for tracking your time, and there are many free tools, such as Toggl, that can help you to accomplish this. Until I see the full scope of a person's master's thesis, for example, it would be impossible for me to figure out a flat fee. Until I see the current level of the work and work through the whole project, it's hard to tell. I might also have to have calls with the client and submit comments or questions to the client. Being paid hourly ensures I don't take on a project that requires a lot of editing for a flat fee and then find myself buried in the weeds. When working on another writer's projects and serving as a proofreader or editor, using an hourly rate with a suggested range of hours is recommended. Ask for a small sample of the piece so you can provide an estimate of a range of hours likely needed for the full work.

Rarely does it make sense for a freelance writer to work on an hourly basis, unless there is a substantial reason to avoid working on a per-project basis. Clients tend to be nervous about working with writers on an hourly basis to begin with, and if you do not feel comfortable working hourly and keeping track of your hours, you can ask more questions about the project, then convert this to a per-piece rate.

This makes it much easier for you to control your time as well as your earnings. Since there are limited hours in a workday that you can work on freelance writing projects, it is much easier to charge a per-piece rate and to batch your projects so you are always working on similar stages of projects at the same time.

You can also work on hybrid projects. Imagine that, you are doing writing and editing for a client. You can charge a per-piece rate for the written content and an hourly rate for the editing. You can always come up with a mix like this or stick strictly to hourly or per-project rate, depending on your individual preferences.

CHAPTER 10

Legal Aspects of Running Your Business

As a freelance writer, it's easy to grow your business from being a hobby that pays you extra cash into a full-blown business. The sooner you start treating your growing endeavor like the company that it is, the easier it will be to keep track of the necessary details. One area I wish I had understood better when I started was the legal aspects of launching and growing a company. In this chapter, you learn about various legal aspects of operating your company and how to understand contracts and other important documents.

As a freelancer, it's always a good idea to get everything in writing. I've found that when I gave the client the benefit of the doubt with a project, I always regretted it and wished I had created a contract.

It's also common for new freelance writers to be nervous about using tools like contracts and nondisclosure agreements (NDAs)—and with good reason, because these are legally binding documents. They are used frequently in the freelancing world to clarify who is responsible for what, and they serve as critical pieces of evidence in the event you need to take legal action against a client who has broken their end of the deal.

tip

An attorney who has experience working with freelancers can help you draft and review documents to get answers to freelance-specific questions.

Understanding Freelance Contracts

Most clients might assume that you don't know what you are doing if you don't have a contract. So to ensure that your clients take you seriously and you look professional, you should use a contract.

Even working on smaller projects with a freelance client should necessitate, at a minimum, a conversation about using a contract. A contract not only protects you legally, but it helps to articulate the terms of the job so you can correct any misconceptions or points of confusion prior to working with a client.

Freelance contracts are also a powerful way to protect yourself if a client fails to hold up their end of the bargain. Most frequently, in freelance contracts, this occurs when a client fails to pay you on time. Your legal contract is your opportunity to remind them of the terms of the contract and, if necessary, to go into litigation to fight for the money you deserve.

While these basic benefits certainly protect you and clarify what will happen between the two of you and who owes whom what, it's also a good idea to have a freelance contract for a number of other issues that can emerge.

Contracts Protect You from "Scope Creep"

A contract is wonderful to refer to when a client requests that you do things that you did not include in your initial estimate. Fail to include everything clearly written in your contract,

tip

If a client pushes back on your escape clause, tell them that it's a standard aspect of your agreements that you hope you never have to use, but it's there to protect both parties.

and you could end up putting in a lot more work than you are being paid for.

Many experienced freelancers have found themselves dealing with scope creep when a client legitimately does not understand that you did not promise them everything under the sun or, in purposeful cases, when the client is trying to take advantage of the freelancer.

Allowing for an Exit Strategy

Another reason to have a contract is to protect yourself if you need to cancel the project. An escape clause is frequently used in freelance contracts to enable you or the client to walk away from the relationship. A cancelation fee is typically due by the client, but otherwise you can walk away scot-free.

What Is a Contract?

A freelance contract is a written agreement between you and the client about all the most important and basic terms of working together. For a contract to be legally valid and clear for all involved parties, it needs to include particular information. Including too many details on a freelance contract could become confusing, but failing to include enough information could put you in a difficult position should you need to enforce the contract.

Some of the items that must be included in a contract include:

▶ The names and addresses of all people and companies involved

▶ A clear outline of what is included, such as the number of revisions, length of the content, whether any graphics will be included, and more; the more detailed you are in this section, the better

tip

A contract is a form of negotiation. It's not uncommon to push back with a contract and to request terms better suited to your needs. Don't be afraid to ask.

▶ The price, including when each payment must be paid and how and if a penalty fee applies for late payments

▶ What happens when either party cancels the project

▶ Who owns the work after the project is completed (In most freelance writing contracts, this will be the client, not you.)

    ▶ If the work can be used in another way than initially intended

    ▶ If you can outsource some of the work or share client details with a third party, such as in a sample

When creating a contract or receiving one from a new client, it's worth the effort to read through each line item and to hire a lawyer for some feedback.

Bringing Up Contracts with a Client

Most of your freelance clients will be familiar with the concept of a contract, so don't be afraid to bring up the topic. Some clients might resist signing a contract on smaller projects. Once a client told me, "If a contract makes you feel better, sure." Most clients, however, are business owners themselves and recognize that contracts are a way to state each person's responsibilities in a written format. For clients who are nervous about contracts, keeping things simple, such as one or two pages, is recommended, as is hiring an experienced attorney who can help you create a contract template that you can use again and again.

Over time, as your freelance business grows, you will likely add more elements to your freelance contract. For example, an element that I added one year into my business was a section in which my clients must initial that they have read my sample work and agree that the work they will receive will be substantially similar in style and tone.

I added this clause after having a negative experience with two clients who used vague feedback terms, such as "I just don't like it," making it impossible for me to fix the project. Asking clients to agree that they have reviewed your samples, and likely your overall style, means there's less chance they will cancel the contract. It also gives them an opportunity to decide if we are not a right fit prior to signing the contract.

Using E-Signatures

You can print your contracts and sign them manually, then scan and email them to the client before storing them on your computer or in the cloud. But the old days of having to get actual signatures on a contract have been made much easier by digital signature services. You can use companies such as HelloSign (www.hellosign.com) and more to get a certain number of free signatures every month or pay for a premium service in which clients can e-sign an unlimited number of contracts. You can easily upload your contract to their service and an email notification is sent to the client to prompt their signature. More complicated freelance client-management programs, such as Dubsado (www.dubsado.com), can also be used for the creation and signing of contracts. Many freelance client-management programs like Dubsado are recommended for intermediate and advanced freelancers who are keeping track of multiple clients with regard to onboarding, contracts, instructions, and more. You might not need something this advanced as a beginner. But no matter how you approach it—through digital signatures or collecting an actual piece of paper that has been signed by the client—always keep a copy of your contract so you can refer to it in case there are questions as the project unfolds. And of course, since the contract is not active until all necessary parties have signed it, wait until you have a signed version from you and the client before beginning work.

What to Do with a Client Who Doesn't Want to Sign a Contract

On smaller jobs, or with clients who have not interacted with many freelancers, it's possible they will fight back and claim you don't need a contract. You can handle this situation by explaining that it helps you keep all your paperwork and instructions in order.

For these projects, a simple one-page contract is probably all you need. If you can explain that the contract benefits and protects both of you, and especially if you make it easy for them to sign it digitally, there's a much higher chance they will take you up on your offer.

Dealing with Breach of Contract

If you have a client who has failed to comply, or breached, the contract, you are within your rights to consider legal action. Litigation, however, is expensive, frustrating, and filled with delays. Whether to move forward with an actual lawsuit by hiring an attorney or filing in small claims court can also be complicated by your physical distance from the client. Deciding whether to file depends on the money at stake in the case or how much staying in the contract would harm you.

Most of the disputes between clients and freelancers have to do with payment. When you have discussed payment terms with the client and they have signed the contract, it can be quite frustrating when you haven't been paid for days, weeks, or months after the invoice was sent.

Many companies operate on net-30 terms, meaning they will pay your invoice within 30 days of receipt. In the digital world, however, payments tend to move more quickly, and there's a strong chance that you'll get paid within two to three weeks after completing the work so long as the client's accounting department doesn't have any other stipulations.

Whether or not there's a substantial amount of money on the line, always attempt other methods of dispute resolution first. Litigation is a last resort, and most clients feel the same way. Unfortunately, you will experience clients at some point who don't want to pay or have so many people working for the company in various departments that it's hard to track down where your money is at. Having a late-fee clause inside your contract can prevent many of these problems from happening more than once. Assessing a $25 or 10 percent fee after a certain date usually discourages the client from paying you late again.

If you do use a late fee, be consistent with it. Giving clients grace time or trying to apply it the third time they've paid you late is likely to be viewed as a problem. Send them a note the day before a late fee applies to explain "I really don't want to add the late fee on here, but per the terms of our contract, the payment is now X days late and a late fee amount will apply at 9 a.m. tomorrow." It's amazing how quickly you can get action when you inform people they're on the hook for more money!

> **tip**
>
> Always increase your chances of success in a contract dispute by referring directly to past communication, like the signed contract, the scope of work, and emails. This helps address any concerns and is much clearer than verbal statements or allegations.

Keep a paper trail of all your requests to receive payment, and provide proof of these in your email or letter to the company. I prefer email to phone calls as your first line of contact, although follow-up calls can help. If necessary, reference the contract regarding payment terms if someone in the chain of command is confused about why there's an issue.

Allow a few weeks for the issue to be sorted out, then send a final notice or consider having a lawyer send a strongly worded letter. These letters are much less expensive than formal litigation. They can also avoid small claims court if the client realizes how serious you are about getting paid. Before deciding your course of action, review your state's laws on small claims court. Usually, cases involving a few thousand dollars or less must be managed there. Note that if you are successful in a small claims case, it can still take some time to get paid, and you might still be chasing the client for a longer period than you wanted.

Often, freelancers discover in the midst of preparing for small claims court or litigation that the cost of hiring a lawyer or taking the time off work to go to court doesn't line up with the possible money paid to you. Attempt other methods first, going up the chain of the command in the company and applying pressure while always submitting evidence and directing the recipient to the terms of the contract.

Understanding Nondisclosure Agreements

Nondisclosure agreements (NDAs) may be requested by some of your clients, particularly those who believe that you might use the information you learned in the course of your project against them later.

A common reason that someone may request a nondisclosure agreement is that you will be learning more about the ins and outs of how they run their business or even their client names. NDAs are quite common in ghostwriting because the client will own the final product and may have strict rules about how you can or cannot use the completed piece. An NDA means that you are not entitled to share information about the product or about the client without their express permission.

The actual terms inside a NDA may vary from one document to another, so it's well worth reading over anything that has been sent to you by a prospective client. In most cases, an NDA is simply the client's way to verify that you will not share insider information you learned during the course of your project or attempt to solicit their own clients that you may be doing work for. This is very common with digital marketing agencies.

A digital marketing agency may have developed the initial relationship with a client, but you will have to learn about this client and possibly even speak to the client in the

▶ Understanding Copyrights in Ghostwriting

Some clients will be fine with attaching your name to the finished work. Most working online, however, are hiring you to write on their behalf. They intend to use your finished work or their edited version of it to make it appear as though they wrote it themselves.

Because of this, these clients will want the copyright to the finished piece. This means that you give up all legal rights to those words. You can't turn around and sell that same article to another client. You might not even be allowed to claim that you wrote the piece at all. For this reason, evaluate this in your rates. Most ghostwriting contracts, whether it's for one article or for a completely ghostwritten book, function in this same manner.

Copyright works differently with your magazine clients. Those clients might demand that your piece be 100 percent original, as in no one else can lay legal claim to it. Some might be open to republishing a piece you've sold before. But always read the fine print in a publication like the *Writer's Market* so that you know what ideas or pieces you can and can't sell when it comes to copyright.

process of writing copy for that company. The digital marketing agency doesn't want you to have the opportunity to use the information you learned to try and form your own relationship with the client and essentially poach that client away from the marketing agency.

Other businesses are more concerned with you learning private details about how they operate their company. Again, read through your NDA to ensure you understand what is being requested of you.

NDAs are quite common and are nothing to be fearful about. They may affect you the most when an NDA states that you are not allowed to share copies of your completed work once the ownership has transferred to the client.

This is very common in a ghostwriting situation because the client wants to own the copyright. You might assume it's OK to share your work samples without getting the client's permission, but this could raise legal issues at worst and cause difficult client relationships at best. Make sure you understand what is being asked of you and retain the services of an attorney if you have further questions about what an NDA means.

Understanding Escrow Services

In lieu of having your own contract, you might have other options to determine who is responsible for what in the freelance project. Using a freelance job board site like Upwork, Guru, or Freelancer allows you to tap into the company's escrow service. Rather than paying you directly, the client adds escrow funds to their account within the project directly. When you have completed the project, those funds will be released to you (you can request them, or the client can release them).

It helps to have a written contract also in place for these bigger projects because of the amount of money on the line and to ensure you have protections if, for some reason, the client falls through. On smaller projects, however, the service does enough in terms of clarifying who is responsible for what. Your client might still ask you to sign a contract or to submit an NDA, but sites like Upwork also keep track of your agreement with the client, so it might not be necessary.

You can still use a contract even if you have set up your project through a freelance job board. In many cases, this might not be necessary but is still an option based on your preference. If you do not use an escrow service, consider asking for upfront payment or a 25 percent of 50 percent deposit to show good faith and to allow you to get started on the project. Some clients won't go for this, but it does not hurt to ask. Most experienced freelance writers require full upfront payment or a deposit, so it's a good idea to have in the back of your mind as you grow.

W-9s and 1099s

Many people are hesitant, and with good reason, about sharing their personal identifying information with someone they don't know. However, in the course of doing business over the internet as a freelancer or even with someone that you meet in person regarding freelance contracts, you will need to share some personally identifying information because the client is attempting to meet their legal obligations.

One common example of this has to do with tax reporting. As of press time, clients are responsible for issuing a 1099 to you at the conclusion of any calendar year in which you were paid more than $600 on their projects. This is true unless the payment was made through a third-party system, such as PayPal, which will also send you a 1099.

PayPal and other third-party sites have their own rules about how and when they will send you a 1099, which further complicates things. As of the time of this writing, PayPal gives you a 1099-K if you do more than $20,000 worth of business or more than 200 transactions through their site. Always check out PayPal to see if that information has changed and to determine whether the client needs to send you a 1099-MISC. This means your client does not need to send you a separate 1099, but of course, you'll have to keep track of whether you will hit such a milestone to render the client's 1099 unnecessary. Upwork also has its own system for sending you a 1099, so do your research before you sign up with any third-party site so you know how to avoid receiving separate 1099s on the same money. See the next section for more information on why this is a problem.

Clients who are collecting W-9s, which include your employer identification number (EIN) or Social Security number, use these details only in the process of creating and dispatching your 1099s at the beginning of a calendar year following a year in which you worked for them. If you are not comfortable sharing your Social Security number, even as a sole proprietor, you can register online for an EIN.

Keep a signed copy of a W-9 with your current address on your desktop or accessible in a locked file in the cloud. This can make it much easier to reference when numerous clients are requesting this same information and eliminating the need for you to print and sign the same document repeatedly. Clients are not attempting to collect your personal information by gathering these details, but it is important that you verify that your records match theirs.

When you receive a 1099 from a client in January of a calendar year, make sure it matches with the money you received from that client from the year prior. This is your opportunity to correct any mistakes before it is filed with the IRS. You should keep copies of all your 1099s from your various clients to rectify your business accounts and to ensure that you are paying taxes appropriately. For more information about W-9s, visit www.irs.gov/forms-pubs/about-form-w-9.

When Should You Collect W-9s from Subcontractors?

If you plan to use other writers or virtual assistants who are involved in carrying out your business or assisting with your clients, make sure you have a W-9 on file for them so you can issue your own 1099 at the end of the year. Use an accounting program to verify which freelancers and/or subcontractors underneath you have passed the $600 threshold, which necessitates you filing a 1099.

Remember that using a third-party payment system that issues their own 1099s eliminates the need for you to do this on your own. In fact, many a tax issue could be avoided by the submission of proper 1099 documents. I have had to go to battle with the IRS numerous times after a 1099 was double issued on the same amount of money, such as a client who paid me through PayPal, then also sent me a separate 1099. Contact your third-party payment processor directly to learn if and when they'll send their own 1099. Most 1099s you receive from a client will be a 1099-MISC, but payment processors send 1099-Ks.

Since that same amount of money was being reported on two separate 1099s, the IRS thought it was unreported income. Have these conversations with your clients up front as well as with your subcontractors so you understand who will and who will not be receiving a 1099.

Do You Need a Business Lawyer?

You want to minimize your expenses as much as possible before you have a proven product, but if you start to get traction with freelance writing projects, or you see that your income has grown dramatically, a consultation with a business lawyer can be helpful.

By default, most freelance writers start as sole proprietors. But as your company grows, this business structure might not be appropriate. A meeting with your accountant and lawyer can help you clarify how to launch and what to consider as you grow. Refer to Chapter 4 for an overview of business structure types.

A connection with a business lawyer is a good idea if you need someone to draft your contract for you or to review ongoing contracts. Minor language edits inside a contract can have major implications for you and your rights. Attorneys are trained to spot these details and provide you with guidance. Even if you don't want to hire a lawyer to review your contract for a $500 project, it might be well worth it for that $20,000 project.

Leverage the freelance economy yourself if you can. You might not need a long-term relationship with a business lawyer who wants to work on retainer, so consider turning to Upwork to post your own job for contract review or similar assistance. Yes, you can even find freelance lawyers online now.

Client Management

P erhaps one of the most challenging aspects for new and emerging freelancers is figuring out how to manage clients. Although the outset of your business will require a focus on getting clients, over time, your business needs will shift to figuring out how to better screen clients and to hire them the right way.

New freelancers often forget that business is a two-way street. Spending most of your time in the process of getting new clients means that it's simple to forget that you have a choice about who you work with as well. Not every client is going to be the right fit for you, a lesson that too many freelancers have had to learn the hard way.

This breaks down into some key concepts, including how to identify an ideal client; negotiating terms with clients, such as rates and deadlines; and knowing how to screen for bad clients. In this chapter, you will learn about these various aspects of client management.

How to Identify an Ideal Freelance Writing Client

Along with identifying who it is not appropriate for you to work with, one of the most important things you can do to grow your freelance business and feel more at peace with your life on a day-to-day basis is to identify your ideal freelance writing client. Your ideal client is a target person whom you are trying to work with. It does not mean that this is a single individual or in a single industry.

Rather, your ideal client is a representation of the types of clients with whom you are the most effective and work the best. Every freelancer may have different characteristics associated with their ideal client, but most freelancers can agree that an ideal client will offer ongoing work, provide you with interesting projects, treat you respectfully, and pay you promptly and well.

You might further narrow down your ideal freelance client by thinking about the kind of industry they are in or the size of their business. The primary purpose of selecting an ideal freelance client is so you can direct your marketing to this individual.

Many freelancers starting off as generalists might not understand the benefits of choosing an ideal freelance client and, therefore, may have marketing that is aimed at everyone and, in fact, no one at all.

Tips to Figuring Out Your Ideal Client

If you haven't already had a great deal of freelancing experience, you need to do a deep dive and think carefully about your ideal client. You are likely to find several patterns or common characteristics.

If you already have an established freelance business, think about the projects that you have enjoyed working on most. What do those clients have in common? The most essential step of identifying your ideal freelance client is knowing how to recognize this individual.

The following questions can help you narrow your selection of an ideal client:

▶ What kinds of projects can this client offer you?

▶ Does this client give you the opportunity to work together on a recurring or repeat basis?

▶ What kind of organization do they run, and what is the size of that business?

▶ How involved is your client in these kinds of projects?

▶ Where is the client located?

▶ What is the pace of work that the client demands?

Every client is going to be a little different, but you need to be familiar with who to target because all your marketing should speak directly to your ideal freelance client. To give you a bit more information, let me describe one of my ideal freelance clients.

After working with hundreds of clients and having the opportunity to learn with whom I worked best, I identified that my ideal client is:

▶ An attorney between age 35 and 55

▶ A male attorney who is either managing or a partner in a small to midsize personal injury, estate planning, or family law firm

▶ Prefers the hands-off approach, knowing that I complete all the work and publish it for them where necessary

▶ Respects my communication boundaries and reaches out to me only if they have an idea for an article or any other kind of issue

▶ Prefers ongoing work where blogs are posted on a regular basis a minimum of two times per week, ideally four to five times per week

This pattern emerged in my business relatively early, but I found that when I directed my marketing to speak specifically to this individual, it became much easier to identify and onboard these clients. You, too, can use the same process of identifying your ideal freelance client. Your ideal freelance client is the type of client who you enjoy working for every day. They are not oppressive or overbearing, and they do not frustrate you. They never miss paying their invoice on time, and you look forward to the opportunity to do repeat work for this client.

Creating an Ideal Client Avatar

Your ideal client avatar is a fictitious person who represents who you want to work with. Having this person in the back of your mind can help you determine if you're attracting the right clients with the right messaging to draw them in.

Consider the following questions for developing a mental picture of the person you want to work with:

- ▶ What industry does this person work in?
- ▶ Does my ideal client fall within a particular age bracket?
- ▶ What does this person look like?
- ▶ What is this person's day to day like?
- ▶ Why does this person need my help?
- ▶ What challenges has this person encountered in the past working with others?
- ▶ What do I envision our communication structure to look like?
- ▶ How will I deal with problems with this client, if they arise?
- ▶ What is the emotional state of my client before they hire me?

> **tip** ⓘ
>
> Think about a past boss or client you enjoyed working with. What qualities did they have that you'd like to see in your freelance writing clients?

The more you can tap into the thoughts of your prospective clients, the easier it will be to sell them on your freelance services. Your clients will feel that you understand them deeply before you even work together.

How to Enhance Your Connection to Your Ideal Client Avatar

To speak more confidently and to narrow your pitches, take your ideal client avatar development to the next level by considering these tips:

- ▶ Give the avatar a name. For example, if you work with designers, the name might be Denise the Designer.
- ▶ Find an appropriate cartoon or stock photo image of this person.
- ▶ Write a mission statement about how your ideal client avatar found you and what they need.
- ▶ When speaking with prospective clients, try to determine whether this person falls in line with your ideal client avatar.
- ▶ Recognize that it's OK to have more than one ideal client avatar, but you're much less effective if you believe that "everyone" is your ideal client.

Of course, we don't live in a perfect world. But it never hurts to imagine what your ideal client might look like, so you can set parameters for yourself on what you will and won't accept in the people with whom you work.

How to Negotiate with Clients

Once you have identified your client base, you'll need to know how to negotiate with them. Even if you have established your baseline rate and had a conversation with a client about the initial scope of process, you should know that negotiations can continue up to the point where you sign a contract.

There are even some cases in which you sign a freelance writing contract and you or the client later decide that what you previously agreed to is no longer applicable and you need to update the terms of the contract. In a sense, this is still a negotiation because you and your client must come to terms of the agreement.

Most new freelance writers struggle with the concept of negotiating with clients. As a new freelance writer, you are so excited about the possibility of working with that client that it is difficult to agree to terms on your end that fully protect you. However, experienced and successful freelance writers regularly negotiate terms and are confident in holding to the terms they have set to work with a client. This is simply doing good business, and it also projects confidence to your prospective freelance writing clients who see you as a professional.

Most people in the business world are familiar with the concept of negotiating and will be willing to do it with you as well. Bear in mind that the negotiation process means that some people will not be the right fit for you. You might get on the phone with someone who appears to be an ideal client, but they have no interest in paying your rates and are expecting a 50 percent reduction.

Rather than haggle with this person, and waste precious minutes or hours, it's better to let these kinds of clients go. Likewise, you might find that the client is difficult or unwilling to agree to other terms, such as turnaround times, revisions, or methods and efforts to communicate.

When negotiating with clients, remember your expertise, talent, and value. Negotiating too much, such as doing away with those precious rates you have worked so hard to figure out, can only hurt you. I have found that in every case in which I had negotiated far too low, I have ended up frustrated and ultimately procrastinating. That means that the final project is not as effective or well written as I would have hoped, and this does not help me or the client. This is why you need to be prepared to negotiate with a rate that is fair to you.

Sometimes it might make sense to include discounts for particular clients. I give discounts to clients who are ordering a bulk project, who are giving me very flexible terms in our working arrangement, or who are signing a retainer to work with me on an ongoing basis.

This is because they are reducing the time I have to spend marketing and giving me peace of mind that I can run my business as efficiently and effectively as possible.

Not every client, however, deserves a discount. There is a good chance that as you grow your freelance writing business, you will continue to interact with people who assume that your rate is always negotiable. If a person pushes back on a rate that you have already presented as the lowest you can possibly accept, it's time to wrap up that conversation and move on.

Some people will never be willing to pay the rates that you want to charge, and as you grow your business and raise your rates accordingly, you will continue to experience this on a bigger and more frequent basis. Don't take it personally, as not every client is right for you.

When a client pushes back or attempts to negotiate rates or terms that are well below what you would normally accept, but you still think there is an opportunity to work together, this is your chance to explain your position. Some clients might not have a clue of all the work that it takes to complete a project.

tip

Prepare for possible negotiations by talking scenarios out loud on your own before a phone call or email with a client. This will help you become more comfortable with what to say if the client pushes back.

They might not realize that it can take you hours to complete the interviews necessary to complete a whitepaper or that your process includes comprehensive edits and rounds of revision. Even if you've already listed this in a written format or previously explained it to the client, the conversation regarding your rates is a good opportunity to reflect on how you created those rates to begin with and why you cannot go any lower. This will also give you a sense of whether this client is someone you can work with or who might be a problem going forward if they attempt to push you on every issue you are trying to agree to.

Warning Signs of Bad Clients

There are several different warning signs of clients who might prove difficult to work with. Your personal willingness to adapt or to work with certain people will look different from another freelance writer, but here are some of the things that can indicate a difficult personality.

Watch out when a client attempts to:

► Abuse their communication with you
► Continue to haggle with you or expect more than what you have promised to do
► Clearly violate the terms of the contract
► Speak to you rudely
► Avoid paying on time

The more you can steer clear of these kinds of clients, the easier it will be to work only with your ideal clients.

Client management can make your life difficult or enjoyable as a freelancer. Remember, you're not an employee, you're a business owner. You have the right to refuse service to people who are difficult to work with, and it's a right you should consider exercising. Many happy business owners who freelance choose to work with clients with whom they share general values and approaches to doing business. This makes life easier and fun!

Making Money and Growing Your Business/ Expertise

As a freelance writer, working on writing projects for clients could represent 100 percent of your time and income, or it might be a mix. What your business looks like is up to you. There are many ways to branch out to grow your income, expertise, and influence as you go. In this chapter, you'll read about some of the most common types of ways to supplement your freelance writing income or existing services so you can continue to scale your business model.

Content Manager

A content manager might have an array of skills to bring to the table, such as knowing how to write great headlines and coordinate many writing projects at once. They should also know how to use specific content systems. For example, a content manager working with a company whose site is hosted on WordPress should be familiar with how to use this software to add content to a website.

A content manager position is most appropriate for companies that create a significant amount of content on a regular basis or work with large teams of freelance writers and editors. A company that wants to create content will often struggle with all the end-to-end steps of creating topics or concept briefs, hiring freelancers, drafting materials, providing feedback, or publishing materials. This is where a content manager comes in.

Project Manager

A digital project manager is responsible for a team of people working on particular projects or ongoing work to ensure that everyone knows their individual duties.

tip

Project management will appeal to those writers who want more variety and client communication mixed into their day.

The project manager also breaks down the project into smaller pieces and keeps the project moving toward the finish line. Often, a project manager is more of a chaos coordinator and works to manage the team.

Over the course of my freelance writing business, I've taken on a few exciting projects as a project manager. I learned a lot about the hiring and training process and used those skills in future jobs or my own business.

If you prefer to be a loner or not have much interaction with a team, working as a project manager is likely not for you. The project manager is in charge of the team and acts as the liaison between the company and other employees or freelancers. You'll often have to interpret messages from one group to the other with special care, which can be a hard role to play.

Virtual Assistant

A virtual assistant, or VA, is like an administrative assistant who works online rather than in an office. Branching out to offer VA services might be right for you if you'd prefer more variety in your day instead of just writing. For some freelancers, the mix of client interaction and focused writing time gives you the chance to grow two businesses—freelance writing and VA—at the same time.

Some VA job postings will ask for a person experienced with writing. Even if the job post doesn't specifically mention writing skills, it's a great talent to bring to the table for a client who might need to rely on your writing expertise from time to time.

VAs might handle tasks for a client's personal life, business, or both. You'll find VAs working in all industries and some who choose to focus on specific tasks or projects because they are highly skilled or just prefer it. I've met graphic design VAs, Pinterest-only VAs, and just about everything in between. Choosing something you're passionate about is perfect to branch out in your freelance writing career.

Some of the most common types of tasks done by VA include:

- ▶ Managing emails
- ▶ Managing a calendar
- ▶ Coordinating travel
- ▶ Scheduling social media
- ▶ Arranging meetings
- ▶ Booking clients for podcasts, webinars, and virtual summits
- ▶ Basic website maintenance

Working as a VA is different from writing, but it might provide some new opportunities to learn. VA are in high demand, and your background as a writer makes you a competitive candidate.

Content Strategist

In the age of digital marketing, companies are recognizing that a whole new kind of expert is needed, whether in-office or virtually. This person is known as a content strategist (CS), a person who plays a variety of roles for the company but ultimately has the responsibility of directing the content marketing. This can include attending conferences, choosing titles, deciding what kinds of content marketing to focus on, overseeing freelance writers and editors, and generally steering the ship. A CS is sometimes in charge of deciding these and then outsourcing the work to a writer on the team.

As a CS, you might provide recommendations to existing team members or other freelancers regarding website copy, brochures, taglines, social media copy, webinar slides, or more. Sometimes a CS acts as a bit of a "writing/editing coach" in giving feedback if they spot a particular pattern where the copy is falling short.

This type of position is most appropriate for an experienced freelance writer who understands why brands need a strategy in the first place. While some content managers might also write, this is mostly a strategic or consulting position in which you're more of a director of overall marketing strategy.

Social Media Manager

The line between a VA and social media manager can get blurred when you initially begin your research into this position. Some VAs don't work on social media, but others will.

A person who brands themselves specifically as a social media manager likely only handles either all platforms used by a client or a specific platform, such as the example of the Pinterest VA mentioned above.

A social media manager should be adept at trends in social media and the related requirements to be successful there. For example, someone familiar with Instagram must be knowledgeable about filters, hashtags, and influencer strategy. Many social media managers who choose to focus on a platform do so because of their own experience or passion for it. This makes it easy for your interest to shine through to prospective clients.

Some of the most common tasks completed by a social media manager include:

- ▶ Reviewing trending topics
- ▶ Providing recommendations for how often a person/company should post on various platforms
- ▶ Writing social media captions
- ▶ Recommending hashtags or other platform-specific material
- ▶ Engaging with other community members or followers on social media

If you love interacting on social media, doing this as a service for clients can help you get paid for something you're already passionate about.

Editorial Services

There are many different terms used for a person who goes through another writer's work and makes comments, edits, or suggestions. These can include copyeditor and proofreader.

In addition, you can provide more general editorial services that may include these functions, as well as substantive, developmental, or line editing.

Copyeditor

Copyediting is the process by which an editor makes formatting changes and grammatical improvements to written material. A person who performs the task of copyediting is usually called a copyeditor.

In many cases, a copyeditor will be the only person, other than the writer of the material, to read the entire text before its publication. The copyeditor's job is to make the copy clear, correct, concise, comprehensible, and consistent. Copyediting typically includes correcting spelling, punctuation, and grammatical errors, as well as making a writer's prose easier to read and understand. Copyeditors also make sure the final text follows a specific style, and usually style guidelines are provided to the copyeditor for this purpose.

Copyeditors also add standardized formatting elements, such as headers, footers, and headlines. These elements of the final publication design must be determined before the publisher can prepare final copy for proofing or before an item can be posted to a website. The copyeditor is expected to see that the text flows well and makes logical sense. A copyeditor looks for missing facts or confused wording, as well as reviewing the text to make sure that it will cause no legal problems for a publisher.

The list of potential clients who need copyeditors is long. Obviously, any publisher of newspapers, magazines, or books requires copyeditors. However, publishers of websites, online materials, and self-published books can also benefit from copyeditors. No matter what size the publisher is, copyediting opportunities are usually available. Some other local organizations that are likely to need copyediting services include:

- ▶ Ad agencies
- ▶ Accountants and accounting firms
- ▶ Individual authors
- ▶ Law firms
- ▶ Corporations
- ▶ Government agencies
- ▶ Public relations firms
- ▶ Professional associations
- ▶ Schools, colleges, and universities
- ▶ Small local businesses
- ▶ College and university students
- ▶ Chambers of commerce

Special skills required for copyeditors include: a good grasp of grammar, knowledge of standard proofreader's marks, and the ability to make written copy clear and concise.

Proofreader

Proofreading involves some of the same work as copyediting but on a more detailed level. In the past, working as an editor or proofreader often referred to working for magazines or newspapers. But as the need for digital content has grown, so too has the demand for editors to keep an eye out for mistakes.

A proofreader for a publisher reviews a proof from the printer, which might have been edited by a copyeditor already. The proofreader checks everything from spelling in the headlines and page numbering to making sure that photos match captions and captions match illustrations. For an online client, however, a proofreader reviews content before it's published live on a website.

In many cases, the proofreader is the last person who sees the text before the printer is authorized to start the press or publish content on a website. So in effect, they are the last line of defense for catching spelling, grammatical, or punctuation errors that may have slipped past the copyeditor.

Working as a proofreader or an editor is an excellent way to expand your services, possibly even making more money with the same clients or adding variety to your workday. It's an easy leap to make because you already possess the writing skills necessary to spot mistakes and to understand the general flow of quality writing.

Proofreading and copyediting are services needed by people who use in-house talent or freelancers to complete projects or even people who write for themselves and want a second pair of eyes.

Most editing work is charged on an hourly basis. This is recommended unless you have an opportunity to review all the work in question before you agree to do it.

Avoiding Mistakes in Your Freelance Writing Business

One of the easiest ways to grow your business is to avoid making preventable mistakes. As a new freelance writer, you'll often feel like you're in new territory, which makes relying on the experience of another writer so helpful. What's included here are my best recommendations to avoid many of the most common problems and challenges experienced by new freelance writers.

Any business owner will go through learning experiences and growing pains. Successful business owners will take those lessons and use them to improve future decisions, contract terms, and client relations. You can speed up your path to success by avoiding these mistakes.

Waiting Too Long to Get Started

The biggest mistake you can make is deciding not to get started if this book has intrigued you at all. Most people fear taking a leap of faith and will hold back from starting a freelance writing career. Some will spend weeks or months doing research, allowing the competition to swoop in and build their own business models.

If you think you have the core skills to succeed as a freelance writer, you should not wait. With so little risk involved in getting started, it's far better to begin pitching to clients and trying to land smaller projects.

In any new venture, it's natural to feel a lack of self-confidence. Most of the aspects of running your business will be new to you, and your subconscious will use all this as an opportunity to convince you that you're in over your head. However, if you keep forging forward and educating yourself about new things, you'll convince your clients that you're worth working with.

It's always going to be based on your individual schedule and your timeline as far as what you want to accomplish in your freelance business. As a teacher to thousands of new freelancers, I often see the same people popping into my group or my YouTube channel every couple of months with new questions about getting started. This signals to me that they still haven't tried to get things going. Life can always get in the way of what you want to achieve, and it can take time to build up a client roster. But I've found both with starting a business and with growing it that small, consistent efforts every day really add up.

How do you eat an elephant? One bite at a time. So break big projects into smaller action steps. With every small step that you accomplish, you build your self-confidence. These are called "stackable wins." It can seem daunting to list "write five writing samples and edit them" on your to-do list for today. It's all too easy to talk yourself out of it and get nothing done. So how about "choose two topics for writing samples" instead? This gives you more time to mull over your ideas and less of a chance to

tip

Set small, manageable goals to launch your freelance writing business. It's much easier to take smaller action steps each day to make progress.

ignore this step. Your writing samples will be better because of it, and you'll benefit from the momentum of accomplishing all these smaller steps stacked on top of one another.

Working for Friends and Family

This can be a tricky situation when someone you know offers you a chance to work together. As a new freelance writer, it's easy to cut through all the hard work of pitching to land your first client. However, this can be a very difficult situation because emotions are involved. I find that it's easier not to work for people I know at all because it removes the emotional tension and keeps the focus on a business relationship.

The best testimonials tend to come from people who you don't know personally. That's because even if a friend hired me to do some work, anyone who knows we were connected before might not take their testimonial as seriously. It doesn't really help my business if my husband's testimonial is the only one I have on my website. It also helps you with your confidence if your first experiences with clients show you that it's not too scary to work with strangers so long as you know your ideal client type and enforce clear boundaries in a contract.

Many people in your immediate circle might be excited to help you start or grow your business. You might be interested in the prospect of helping them with a project they don't want to do or don't have time to do. This is a best-case scenario when working for someone you know. In the worst-case scenario, a friend or family member might not have any clue about market rates for freelance projects. They might assume that they're entitled to a steep discount because they know you. And worst of all, if the business relationship goes south, your friendship or relationship could be damaged.

Another possible downside to working with someone you know is it can be hard to separate your personal and business life. For example, consider the tension that could be created if you're working for a friend whom you're connected to on social media and you're late on their project. If that friend sees you posting pictures of your latest outing when their project is overdue, bad blood can ensue.

This is not to say that you should never work with friends or family. But I've seen far too many situations in which the business and the personal relationship eroded, so I've chosen to keep my personal and private life separate. Having freelance friends who might be able to help your loved ones and acquaintances with projects is helpful.

> **tip** ⓘ
>
> You can work successfully with friends and family, but be prepared with crystal clear contracts and outstanding communication on boundaries if you want to maintain the personal relationship.

If you choose to work with someone you know in this manner, go the extra step of explaining your process. Someone who doesn't fully understand your world as a freelance writer might need help understanding that you don't work for them alone and that you could be busy with multiple projects at once. Before committing to work together, offer a basic overview of what they can expect.

Conflicts of Interest

Depending on your line of freelance writing work, you could encounter conflicts of interest. You'll learn that different clients have varying levels of tolerance about these conflicts.

For example, as a writer for attorneys, I never work with two attorneys in the same geographic area. It would be an ethical issue for me to support two competing businesses and possibly even take what I'm learning from one to help another. Imagine that one of my clients invests in a course for me to take so I can help them improve their blog. If I use the information I learned to also help their direct competitor, it's not fair and can easily be avoided.

If you're working in a more general industry, it's not uncommon for clients to ask, "how many other dentists are you writing for?" In general, these localized industries won't be too concerned if you're writing for one in Texas and one in Utah, since they each have their own clients. But if you're working for a company that does website design and you get a writing offer from a similar company with a nearly identical target market, be careful with how you proceed, as this could be interpreted by the client as a conflict of interest.

In general, my rule of thumb is that I don't worry much about conflicts of interest unless something I'm thinking about doing could harm a current or a prospective client.

A common conflict of interest question is raised if you worked for a company in the past in which you became connected with that company's clients. What happens if one of those clients reaches out to you and wants to do business with you? Much of this depends on whether you signed a noncompete agreement with your former company. As a ghostwriter, there's little chance that your former employer would even know you're doing the writing, but make sure you read through your former employment contracts to make sure you're not obligated to steer clear for a certain period.

Conflicts of interest or ethical concerns can emerge in other ways, too. There are industries that you might not feel comfortable writing for. For example, many writers will happily take on many kinds of projects, but you'll never find them writing about recreational drug use, gambling, politics, or religion. As with many things in your freelance writing business, most of the decision is up to you.

Taking on Low-Paying, High-Stress Clients

As a new freelance writer, you'll probably be excited when anyone offers you work. But this also means that it's far too easy to end up in a cycle working for clients who don't pay you enough.

Considering the relatively low minimum wage and the challenges of leaving your house to pursue other income in a more traditional part-time job, an offer to pay you 5 cents per word might seem like a good deal.

But then when you sit down and factor in how much work you had to do to land that client, research the ideas, write, and complete the work, you realize you might be making minimum wage or less. Charging a flat rate for pieces when you start might be easier if you have an idea of how long it might take you to do something. As a newbie, it's common to accept lower rates than what you'd take if you'd been in business for a decade. But the truth is that you can't live on low wages forever, and it also doesn't reflect your growing experience and talent.

As your freelance writing ability and client list grows, so too will your rates. Don't beat yourself up if you suddenly come to the realization that you're charging way too little. Either fire these clients once you've replaced the income with someone better or tell the client that your rates are going up, including an effective date, and give them the choice to pay your higher rates or to move on.

▶ Knowing Your Value: A Cautionary Tale

There's a saying in the freelance writing world that the lowest-paying clients will also be the most demanding. I have found this to be true. Consider this example from one of my earliest clients. I was excited to be paid $8 for a 300-word article when I launched. I wrote ten articles per week for this client and brought in $80 a week. Since I was just coming from a low-paying job, I thought this was great. I was able to keep up that momentum for a few weeks until I realized just how much time it was taking me. During that period, the client had also become more demanding. Now they wanted more bells and whistles added to the project, like images, subheads, and meta descriptions. But despite adding all these requirements, the pay did not change.

Thinking that it was reasonable, I asked for a pay bump to accommodate the extra requests. The company responded by telling me that I was lucky to have a steady writing gig. In hindsight, it's embarrassing that I thought cranking out $8 a piece was a great deal. It was burning me out and paid me far less than I deserved.

As a business owner, you must develop thick skin and the ability to put all your cards on the table. You might suggest what you consider to be a more than reasonable offer only to have the client fire back that they'll never pay it. This is always a gamble but one that is worth it. I had one client for four years. I never raised their rate because they were easy to deal with, always paid on time, and were so consistent with weekly work. But once I explained to them that my rates were going up, they backed out and canceled the contract. While it was scary to go through that, I was able to replace them with a better-paying client in a matter of weeks.

I've seen so many new freelance writers turn into veteran freelance writers with the same client roster—or worse, new clients they've brought on at the same abysmal rates. Remember that as a business owner you're also paying your own taxes. You have to ensure you make enough money from your clients to pay your bills, expenses, and taxes. Don't undercut yourself because not only will you fail to make enough money but you'll also suffer from lack of confidence and likely end up in a cycle in which you work with the same style of bad client over and over.

Plagiarized Work

Most people know that you can get in a lot of trouble in school with copied work. In the business world, there's no faster way to burn bridges as a freelance writer. Because so many people are hiring freelance writers to help them with online content, there are plenty of ways to check whether you have accidentally copied someone else's words in your project.

This is also important to know if you intend to hire subcontractors to write for you, because you want to check that they haven't copied anyone else's work, either, whether intentionally or accidentally.

Tools like Copyscape can tell you whether something you've written is similar or identical to anything else on the internet. I strongly recommend it because it can be harmful to websites to have what's known as "duplicate content."

Aside from the fact that your clients will be mad if you copied another person's words, you could cause their site to suffer in search engine rankings because Google and other search engines ding websites with duplicated content. Copyscape is a minor investment but one that's well worth it.

As you write more often and in the same subject areas, you also want to make sure you don't copy yourself. Having written hundreds of blogs in one subject area, sometimes I've found that I've used the same phrase from years ago. I want to avoid that if it's on a page that is still live on a client's website.

That's why Copyscape is worth the several cents per search just to make sure you're in the clear. If you have clients asking for "100% original copy," what they mean is that your search through Copyscape yields no similar results.

Aside from getting caught due to these commonly used tools, it's a bad idea to copy anyone else's ideas. It's bad business, and even if you're lucky enough to slide by once, why would you want to? Eventually, your clients will find out and be disappointed, and you will have lost their business and any jobs they might have referred your way. This is a lazy way to approach your freelance writing business and not ever worth the risk. I've worked with dozens of clients who came to me after they discovered that another writer was plagiarizing, so just assume your clients are checking your work for originality. Having a unique style and approach to each project makes you more marketable anyway.

Doing "Free Work" for Exposure

You'll find plenty of clients online but even offline who will offer you "exposure." This is a fancy way of saying that you won't get paid well or at all for your work, but other clients might see your work and decide to hire you. You should make the decision about whether to work for free based on your gut feeling and financial situation, but rarely do these gigs lead to anything.

If *The New York Times* offered you a chance to write for them for free, this could be worth the clips that you can direct other clients to. Readers might spot the link to your website or Google you and decide to hire you. But increasingly, some companies that make vague promises about how many "hundreds" or "thousands" might see your work are using this as an opportunity to get free work from you.

Remember that most companies who offer you free exposure will not be at the level of *The New York Times*. Many are websites that are rarely visited, or worse, are generating ad revenue for themselves based on that material that you have written, but you'll never see a cut of it.

I did "free" work for a company for two years when I started. The site did have great exposure—more than 100,000 readers landing on their pages, and many of those pages featured my articles. I only wrote one article a week during that time, and it was based on my personal experience, so the articles were easy and quickly written. Establishing my name as a writer online and having so many clips did help to demonstrate that I was a professional writer, but I eventually outgrew that site and left it. Although I got a few leads out of it, none of them were worth the time I invested, and I quit because of it.

One option you can consider if you're thinking about taking an "exposure" gig is to offer short-term help, say for a few articles or for a month. Then you can re-evaluate and decide if this is worth your time. Often, these exposure gigs don't pan out, and your time is much better spent marketing for paid gigs using other means.

If you take on multiple clients who don't pay you, you're giving up all your time, energy, and talent and not getting anything for it. Be cautious of any company that offers you no pay or extremely low pay in exchange for the possible exposure.

I've seen a freelance joke that we don't ask to pay our dentist, lawyer, car mechanic, or anyone else with exposure. This joke has merit because we shouldn't be expected to give up our talent and time for no pay.

Overbooking Yourself

It's a new freelance writer's dream—and worst nightmare—to be so overbooked that you miss deadlines and upset current clients. There's no easy well to tell what your own schedule should look like since this depends on the time you have available. One freelance writer might be comfortable cranking out ten articles a day whereas another feels totally exhausted after doing the research for one. This is why making your samples can help you figure out what's in your wheelhouse and what isn't.

If you start to feel like you're barely keeping up with your projects or that you're making mistakes and clients are making comments about it, this is a key sign that you could be overbooked.

There's an upside to being overbooked once you dig yourself out of the weeds: It's time to raise your prices. There's obviously a demand for your services when you have so many clients that you can't keep up with your current projects, so it might be time for you to raise your rates for any new clients you take on.

It can take some time to find your footing as a freelancer, and you're likely to realize your own limits just after you've passed them. It's a good reminder to decide how best to handle the situation so that it doesn't happen again. If you're overbooked, you might need to log some extra time in front of the computer, let a client go, or raise your rates immediately since there's such a high demand for your talents.

Not Putting Enough Time into Your Samples

Your pitch and samples are crucial in your freelance writing business; you simply will not be able to get clients without them. Your samples speak volumes about your talent and writing style. Even if your samples are not perfectly aligned to the project at hand, clients want to know what your writing looks like.

If there's one comment I hear again and again from my new clients, it's that they loved the style of my writing samples. This seems to clinch the deal for them to sign the contract, which speaks to just how important it is for you to make your samples blow your clients out of the water.

Your samples deserve your time and respect. If I told you that a few hours of your invested time could lead to hundreds or thousands of dollars in future returns, you'd be more motivated to make the effort, right? This is why you need to block off some time for your samples.

You're probably like I was when I launched my freelance writing business. I'd never been paid before to write anything, so I had no idea what to do to convince clients that I could handle these writing projects.

I did some research about the kind of writing I wanted to do and figured that since I didn't have published clips I could make some up. I was honest with my clients that these weren't published anywhere online, but since plenty of freelance writers are ghostwriters who don't get direct credit for what they've created, the clients who hired me on these samples didn't care.

I created three SEO blog-writing samples about topics I cared about and for the industry in which I wanted to write. I often recommend to students of mine that this is a good route to pursue. You could also choose to create three different styles of writing to showcase your versatility. You might create a technical, funny, and professional sample so you can pick and choose which one or ones are most applicable to the gig you're submitting for. Those three samples landed me thousands of dollars in gigs, so the five hours I spent researching topics, writing, and editing were well worth it. Since you'll likely be using the same samples over and over, make the effort to work hard on them. Cutting it short and whipping something up quickly could block you from getting offers on great projects, so make sure your writing samples are the highest quality you can offer.

All too often, I've been on the hiring end of a project in which the submitted samples were poorly written or even contained errors. A client who is hiring you to write for them personally or for their business will not forgive this level of sloppiness. Let your samples sing and showcase your best work. Hire a professional editor if you have to, but block out several hours to complete your samples so you have the best possible chance of landing the gig and impressing the client.

Trying to avoid the newbie mistakes in this chapter can save you a lot of time and headaches and make sure that you are on the path to growing your company quickly and professionally.

Coaching and Mentoring Your Way to Success

I n 2012, when I started my freelance business, I agonized

for weeks over buying a $20 ebook about freelance writ-

ing. Did I have what it took? Would this be a waste of

money? What if I hated the book?

As a new writer, it's common to hesitate spending money

on anything. As a business owner, you take on a lot of

responsibility to manage your company, and suddenly that pressure might make you hesitant about hiring anyone to help or purchasing books and courses to give you a leg up. However, as a buyer of this book, you're one step ahead of where I was when I started.

I waited for a long, long time before I hired a mentor. I regret doing that because I think I would have grown my business much faster if I'd simply followed the proven path of someone else. When I did find that mentor, I purchased everything she had for sale. I read her blog and every new post. I sent her emails and asked questions, made suggestions for new products she could create, and interacted with her in the comments section.

This mentor helped me scale my business so much because she had built her business exactly the way I wanted to. She was a great role model.

A coach can be a worthwhile investment when this person has traveled the road you are on and has insights that can help you out of sticky situations quickly. Having someone to whom you ask questions and speak with will also help you bust through mindset issues.

Another aspect of launching or growing your business that can be fast-tracked with a coach is accountability. When working for yourself, you are the sole person responsible for getting things done. And if you've ever made a commitment to yourself January 1st and gave up a few days later, you know just how hard it is to be accountable to yourself. Checking in with a coach can help you avoid the common timeframes in which you'd usually give up.

> **tip**
>
> When looking for a mentor, look for someone who has already built what you want to achieve. There are several freelance writing coaches who stopped writing years ago or only write a handful of articles per month. While this is not to say you can't learn something from them, I recommend finding a mentor who is still in the trenches so you know they are keeping on top of current trends and tips and can offer advice from the perspective of someone who is experiencing the same level of success you want to achieve. The shortcut to success is finding a proven path from a person who has been there and can help you avoid many missteps.

Types of Coaching Arrangements

Not every form of coaching is right for everyone. Knowing what works for you and what doesn't can help you narrow the search for the right person to assist you. As a person who was coached by professional freelancers, and as a coach for new and fast-growing freelancers

▶ Trust Your Gut

Be careful when choosing coaches who advise you about following their way rather than providing a strategy customized for you. There's a big difference between these two approaches, and you could lose a lot of money working with a coach who wants you to follow a specific system that isn't meant for you.

As an example, one set of freelance mentors I worked with were adamant about not settling into a niche. As you discovered in Chapter 6, having a niche enabled me to become an expert in a few select subject areas and to market myself more effectively. When hiring a coach, trust your instincts. If you feel firmly about something, hold your ground. This is why it matters that you find a coach who wants to help you build your business your way.

myself, I've been involved in every one of these coaching arrangements. Each one has pros and cons.

Courses with Limited Support from the Coach

You might find that your budget and needs align perfectly with investing in a course that has some limited support from the coach or creator. A sign-up bonus for a course on a particular marketing strategy, for example, might come with a 30- or 45-minute call with the coach.

Or part of your enrollment might include a group call scheduled out over a series of weeks. Since there's limited interaction with the coach or course creator, much of the responsibility is on you. However, getting some insight or interaction with the coach can work if you plan to clear up just a few questions.

If you're the type of person who tends to sign up for things and then not follow through, this method of coaching is not recommended. You'll likely fall behind quickly and skip the included calls or coaching since you haven't reviewed the material. You would benefit more from the level of accountability provided by mastermind or one-on-one coaching.

> **tip** ⓘ
>
> Research as much as you can about the person you're planning to hire before working together. Most one-on-one coaches will offer you a free strategy session so you can see if you're a fit. This initial meeting will help you determine your personality match, and even if it does not work out, you should still get some action steps to apply right away.

Coaching can get expensive. The more time you spend interacting in small groups or one on one with a coach, the higher the price tag. Coaching with limited support comes with the lowest investment and might be your entry point to the world of coaching.

Strategy Sessions

If you don't need long-term support, a strategy session with a professional can help. Imagine, for example, that you're not sure of the tax savings of being an S corp vs. an LLC. A one-hour strategy session with an accountant can help you get direct answers without having to pay for retainer services until you're ready or need them. Strategy sessions can also help you with emergency issues, specific problems, or concerns on just a handful of things.

tip

Be coachable. If you're not willing to receive feedback and consider ideas, you're halting your own growth. Choosing the right person as a mentor can make a big difference in your ability to take action and get results. If you're too focused on making excuses, you'll end up frustrated with the coaching relationship. Take ownership of your decisions instead.

You can use strategy sessions for contract reviews, marketing questions, help scaling your business, discovering how to hire a virtual assistant to help with your workload, and more. These can be as expensive as a single course or less expensive, depending on the coach and the overall time investment. Make sure you seek out the services of someone who is likely to know your situation and the questions you have. As an example, I've worked with and built many teams of freelancers, so people who purchase strategy sessions with me often want help hiring their first VA or figuring out what to outsource. As with all forms of coaching, do your homework first and make sure the person you're thinking of working with has the right expertise.

Mastermind/Group Coaching

This form of coaching is one step up from purchasing a course or book and reading through the materials. Mastermind coaching involves a group of like-minded professionals sharing their concerns and problems in a shared setting and getting feedback not just from the coach but also from the other group members.

A mastermind works well if you enjoy engaging with others, since you can learn just as much from other people's experiences as you can from the coach. This is also well suited to you if you're concerned about the isolation typically linked to writing. A weekly mastermind meeting can help you by allowing you to interact with your peers and to feel like you're part of a community.

In a mastermind group, you might have weekly, biweekly, or monthly sessions over a set period. Your investment will be more than what you'd pay for a course alone, but you get the blend of the instructor's teaching and insight from other group members. Often, a mastermind call or meeting will be conducted with the coach leading a portion of the training on a specific topic and then spot-coaching each person on the call for 10 to 15 minutes.

Masterminds can include a general group of people hoping to achieve more with their life, goals, or business. However, you can also find freelance masterminds, which will be more tailored to the kinds of issues and concerns you have within your own business.

Masterminds will not be a good fit if you have extremely limited time or find it frustrating to listen to everyone else's questions if they are not relevant to you. This is why a more focused mastermind group of only freelancers is recommended. You might have less in common with a lawn and garden groundskeeper looking to grow his business with direct mail in a general mastermind group than you do with a virtual assistant in a freelance-specific group looking for tips on how to use LinkedIn.

Regarding time, if you have a set working schedule at a day job or child-care issues, and the mastermind call is scheduled each Thursday at 3 P.M. when you can't get away, this is a poor investment. These groups run anywhere from six weeks to a full year, so it's smart to ask questions first to ensure you'll be getting the most out of the program.

Before investing in a mastermind, which can run from a few hundred dollars up to six figures for groups with legendary entrepreneurs or experts, do your research. Understand what you're paying for and for how long. Also, have a conversation with the group facilitator to check for personality conflicts.

Masterminds can be powerful tools for learning since if you're in the right group, you can benefit from the coaching given to all other members. You'll walk away with support for your individual concerns while also getting the benefit of all the learning you gain from other members and the coaching they receive.

One on One

One-on-one coaching is easily the most expensive, but this is because you're getting the instructor's undivided attention. You don't share your phone calls or in-person meetings with anyone else.

One-on-one coaching involves a big commitment in terms of time, focus, and finances on your part, so it's recommended only for those who want to fast-track their success with a deep dive or who have time in their schedule. Most new freelancers cannot afford a one-on-one coach outside of strategy sessions, so it's fine to table this level of support until you're overbooked, thinking of changing niches or marketing channels, or need some other type of specific help.

Like a mastermind group, this form of coaching can have varying levels of investment and time commitment. A good coach will challenge you, and that experience is amplified when you work with a coach one-on-one. Be prepared to hear some things that might be difficult or outside your comfort zone. That's a big reason why people hire a one-on-one coach to begin with, so it's frequently part of the experience.

Ultimately, you should view coaching and mentoring as an investment rather than an expense. While you are putting forth money to learn and grow, this kind of business consulting can propel you to the next level much faster. Most coaches will enable you to earn your investment back quite quickly if you're implementing the tips the right way.

Final Thoughts

This book has given you a broad overview of what the market for freelance writers looks like and what you can expect if you choose to launch this kind of business. As you go forward, be open to the new things you'll need to learn, remain critical of your own work, continue marketing on a regular basis, and be firm in the boundaries you set with clients. Being a freelance writer is an exciting and interesting profession when it's the right fit for you, and the demand has never been better. Don't hesitate to take action if you're ready to put your writing skills to use!

Freelance Writing Resources

They say you can never be rich enough or thin enough. While that's arguable, we firmly believe you can never have enough resources. Therefore, we're giving you a wealth of sources to check into, check out, and harness for your own personal information blitz.

These sources are tidbits—ideas to get you started on your research. They are by no means the only sources out there, and they should not be taken as the ultimate answer. We have done our research, but businesses tend to move, change, fold, and expand. As we have repeatedly stressed, do your homework. Get out there and start investigating!

Accountants/Tax Support Who Have a Focus on Freelance/at-Home Business Returns

Accountable Solutions: https://costamesataxreturn.com/

Finance University for the Self-Employed https://fuse.teachable.com/p/fuse

Susan Lee, Accountant https://www.freelancetaxation.com/

CPA for Freelancers https://www.cpaforfreelancers.com/

Brass Taxes https://brasstaxes.com/

Advice on Magazine Writing/Magazines to Pitch To

Writer's Market: http://www.writersmarket.com
 (*Writer's Market* also has great resources for finding a literary agent.)

Freelance Writing Job Boards/Lead Sources

FlexJobs: www.FlexJobs.com

Freelance Writing Jobs: www.freelancewritinggigs.com

ProBlogger: www.ProBlogger.com

Upwork: www.upwork.com

We Work Remotely: www.WeWorkRemotely.com

nDash: www.nDash.co

General Freelancing Advice

Ed Gandia, High Income Business Writing: https://b2blauncher.com/

Yuwanda Black, Inkwell Editorial: www.inkwelleditorial.com

Tools to Help You Become a Better Writer or Check Your Work

Copyscape: www.copyscape.com

Grammarly Editing Tool: www.Grammarly.com

Hemingway App: www.hemingwayapp.com

Upwork Advice

BetterBiz Academy: http://www.betterbizacademy.com/blog?category=Upwork%20advice

Six Figure Writing Secrets: http://sixfigurewritingsecrets.com/writing-on-upwork/

Mastering Your Freelance Life Facebook Group:
   https://www.facebook.com/groups/483154598732958

Writing Advice for Developing Online Copy/Content

Backlinko: www.backlinko.com

Glossary

1099: Tax document that explains that you did contract or freelance work for a company. You should receive these documents once a year in January or February for work done the year prior. For your subcontractors who earn more than $600 in a calendar year from you, you need to fill out one and file it with the IRS.

Client: Your customer, with whom you have a contractual relationship to deliver freelance writing materials.

Contract: Your written agreement between the freelance writing client and yourself, outlining the terms and deadlines of your arrangement.

Deadline: The time to turn in materials to your client or the due date.

Freelancer: An independent contractor who gets paid by specific companies for doing a specific task or project.

Ghostwriter: Someone that writes for another person and receives money but no byline for the work.

Job board: A place where clients post possible jobs and you respond with a pitch, samples, and any relevant questions.

Index